What Your Colleagues Are Saying . . .

"How fortunate we are as educators to have this brilliant collaboration between Lois Lanning and Tiffanee Brown on Concept-Based Literacy lesson development! To read their deep thinking and practical applications to Concept-Based lesson design, is to realize the critical nature of each student's conceptual understanding and ability to transfer. This book, as well as Dr. Lanning's earlier book (2013) Designing a Concept-Based Curriculum for English Language Arts, *are cutting-edge. Literacy is not a decontextualized drill of skills or learning just about 'a book.' You will highlight, ponder, and tab as you read about the design of Concept-Based Literacy lessons. You will feel the excitement of this intellectual and engaging approach to teaching and learning. You will create your own exciting lesson plans and will know this is the holistic literacy approach you have been searching for. All students deserve the best literacy instruction—and this IS the BEST."*

—H. Lynn Erickson
Author and Consultant

"How do we create 'thinking' classrooms and put theory into action? Templates to build lessons, rubrics to guide our thinking, and examples upon examples are used to help us transform rather than replace what we say and do in our classrooms. This is the 'how to' book that will be the treasured resource for 21st century educators."

—Connie Walser, Consultant Teacher Grades 6–8
Bay View School
Burlington, WA

"Concept-Based Literacy Lessons *is a user-friendly text that invites deeper thinking. Even though I lack familiarity with Concept-Based Curriculum, this book provided ample explanation and support and made me want to know more. This is definitely a title I will suggest to our reading coach and ELA faculty."*

—Melissa A. Campbell, Fourth-Grade Classroom Teacher
Williams Avenue Elementary School
Fort Payne, AL

"This is an excellent book for teachers at all levels of experience. Each time I felt a bit of confusion about how I would incorporate this into my teaching, there was an example or story that helped me. These moments are strategically placed to help teachers understand that they can do this type of work; it just requires a shift in thinking. I would like to use this to help teachers create lessons to foster understanding and transfer."

—Barbara Smith, Reading Teacher 3–6
Cutchogue East Elementary School
Cutchogue, NY

"Concept-Based Literacy Lessons *delivers what it promises. The easy-to-read chapters lead the teacher from the excitement of understanding Concept-Based Curriculum back to the classroom with concrete examples and tools to design Concept-Based lessons. It's the all-too-often skipped step in creating meaningful change."*

—Kathleen Swift, High School English Teacher
Newtown High School
Sandy Hook, CT

"This is a fantastic resource for teachers eager to learn how to incorporate Concept-Based learning in their literacy classrooms. By providing a clear unit framework, a wealth of concrete examples of lessons, engaging activities, and coaching tips to apply to your own planning, this book enables you to add a new dimension to your instruction while still maintaining ownership of your own teaching."

—Caity Lehman, Grade 5–7 English Subject Coordinator
Colegio Anglo Colombiano
Bogotá, Colombia

"It is well understood that both achievement and income gaps largely disappear between racial groups when factoring in literacy level. We know that our schools must be producing careful thinkers, close readers, and concise writers in order to address the equity issues in our country. But, we have not found a way to translate this understanding into the daily learning experiences of our children . . . until now. Concept-Based Literacy Lessons *finally provides teachers with the fundamental learning design and array of strategies that are necessary to help each and every child develop critical literacy skills and understandings. Moving beyond proficiency on standardized literacy assessments, students educated based on the elements of this book will learn to how to leverage their voices, written and oral, in support of their own big ideas. They will understand the true power of being truly literate!"*

—K. C. Knudson, Assistant Superintendent
Anacortes School District 103
Anacortes, WA

"The growing consensus among educators of the need for deeper learning and more meaningful lesson design has sparked much in the way of instructional theory and comparatively little in the way of practical instructional support. Lanning and Brown shift the focus to how. This book offers teachers a timely and straightforward approach to the design of dynamic learning experiences that support learning transfer, investigation, and meaning creation."

—Joanne McEachen and Matt Kane
Authors of *Measuring Human Return*
The Learner First

"Concept-Based Literacy Lessons: Designing Learning to Ignite Understanding and Transfer, Grades 4–10 *provides us firsthand experiences in developing and teaching effective Concept-Based units and lessons. Lanning and Brown have created this brilliant pathway that incorporates model lessons and scaffolds to effectively support educators in getting to the practicality of 'what does this looks like on a daily basis?' while allowing for teachers' creativity, passions, and expertise to be honored. This book is like the 'user's guide' to Concept-Based, and will lead you step-by-step to create rich, deep learning experiences that engage our students' hearts and minds."*

—Mischelle Darragh, Principal
Sedro-Woolley School District, Sedro-Woolley, WA
Certified Concept-Based Trainer

"Where other resources on the market focus on theory alone, Lois Lanning and Tiffanee Brown's newest book provides teachers with a practical approach to guide literacy lesson design. Co-authors Lanning and Brown emphasize the critical importance of a Concept-Based classroom that blends both inquiry and explicit skill instruction so that students learn to transfer their ideas across content areas. The model lessons and 'Snapshots' will inspire teachers who want to design purposeful lessons that cultivate students' conceptual understandings."

—Lorrie Rodrigue, Superintendent
Newtown Public Schools, Newtown, CT

Concept-Based Literacy Lessons

To teachers who strive to do their best for their students each and every day and to our families whose support enables us to follow our passion.

Concept-Based Literacy Lessons

Designing Learning to Ignite Understanding and Transfer, Grades 4–10

Lois A. Lanning

Tiffanee Brown

CORWIN

CORWIN
A SAGE Publishing Company

FOR INFORMATION:

CORWIN
A SAGE Company
2455 Teller Road
Thousand Oaks, California 91320
(800) 233-9936
www.corwin.com

SAGE Publications Ltd.
1 Oliver's Yard
55 City Road
London EC1Y 1SP
United Kingdom

SAGE Publications India Pvt. Ltd.
B 1/I 1 Mohan Cooperative Industrial Area
Mathura Road, New Delhi 110 044
India

SAGE Publications Asia-Pacific Pte. Ltd.
18 Cross Street #10-10/11/12
China Square Central
Singapore 048423

Acquisitions Editor: Ariel Curry
Development Editor: Desirée A. Bartlett
Senior Editorial Assistant: Jessica Vidal
Production Editor: Amy Schroller
Copy Editor: Ellen Howard
Typesetter: Hurix Digital
Proofreader: Caryne Brown
Indexer: Judy Hunt
Cover Designer: Alexa Turner
Marketing Manager: Margaret O'Connor

Printed in the United States of America

Printed by Ashford Colour Press Ltd, Gosport, Hants PO13 0FW

Library of Congress Cataloging-in-Publication Data

Names: Lanning, Lois A., author. | Brown, Tiffanee, author.

Title: Concept-based literacy lessons : designing learning to ignite understanding and transfer grades 4-10 / Lois A. Lanning, Tiffanee Brown.

Description: Thousand Oaks, California : Corwin, [2019] | Includes bibliographical references and index.

Identifiers: LCCN 2018037335 | ISBN 9781544318578 (paperback : alk. paper)

Subjects: LCSH: Language arts—Correlation with content subjects—United States. | Interdisciplinary approach in education—United States. | Curriculum planning—United States.

Classification: LCC LB1576 .L3379 2019 | DDC 375/.001—dc23 LC record available at https://lccn.loc.gov/2018037335

Contents

List of Figures and Tables by Chapter

Chapter 4

Chapter 5

Acknowledgments

Our numerous school experiences with colleagues and students shaped the thinking that went into writing this book. Even though we can't name all the places or people individually, both authors acknowledge how each encounter deepened and awakened in us new understandings about the complexities of literacy teaching and learning. Our journey continues.

We would like to acknowledge specifically those who directly contributed to this book. They include the many outstanding educators in Newtown Public Schools, Newtown, CT. The school system is on a quest to systematically advance students' conceptual understanding across subjects and school levels. The district leadership and staff have "the right stuff" and were a joy to work with over the course of several years. Their feedback and encouragement on ideas presented in this book were inspiring.

We also thank the thoughtful and innovative teachers from Burlington-Edison School District in Burlington, WA, who are striving to design student-centered and idea-centered learning experiences for *all* students. To the seventh- and eighth-grade English language arts team, Nolan Harron, Helen Hollister, and Jim Palmer, thank you for your collaboration and for serving as thought partners on this journey to transform literacy learning for our students. Your model unit will inspire others. And, to Connie Walser, Special Education teacher, thank you for sharing your testimonial about the power of co-planning to ensure equitable access to a quality core Concept-Based Curriculum. The students in Burlington-Edison are so lucky to have you as their teachers. We mean that!

To all of the Concept-Based students, such as Makenzie, thank you for sharing your hearts and minds with us as you engage in the Concept-Based learning experiences that your teachers plan. Your enthusiasm and continuous growth are what keeps us going!

And, we cannot go without expressing our gratitude to David Ford for the info-cartoons that capture the essence of each chapter. Not only was David fun to work with, but, as a former school principal, he "gets" Concept-Based and was able to convert words into images with amazing understanding.

For their support, encouragement, and ongoing advice, we are grateful to those in our Corwin "family." The patience and humor of Desiree Bartlett and Jessica Vidal kept us going. Thank you to Amy Schroller, Brian Grimm for keeping our timeline on track, and to Alexa Turner for the perfect cover and interior design. This book would never have come to fruition had it not been for Ariel Curry, our Acquisitions Editor, who was not only generous with her time but open to the ideas we value. Finally, Ellen Howard expertly and efficiently combed the manuscript for errors, picking up random missing commas and other slip-ups. We actually enjoyed our back-and-forths with her!

Publisher's Acknowledgments

Corwin gratefully acknowledges the contributions of the following reviewers:

Jessica Baldwin, 10th and 11th Grade ELA Teacher
Toombs County High School
Lyons, GA

Melissa A. Campbell, 4th Grade Classroom Teacher, Lead/Mentor Teacher in Mathematics
Williams Avenue Elementary School
Fort Payne, AL

Anne Faulks, 7th/ELA/Teacher
Appling Middle School
Bartlett, TN

Clint R. Heitz, Instructional Coach
Bettendorf Community Schools
Bettendorf, IA

Caity Lehman, Grade 5–7 English Teacher, MYP English Subject Coordinator
Colegio Anglo Colombiano
Bogotá, Colombia

Lena Marie Rockwood, Assistant Principal
Revere High School
Revere, MA

Valeria Ruff, 7th grade ELA teacher
Druid Hills Academy
Charlotte, NC

Barbara Smith, Reading Teacher 3–6
Cutchogue East Elementary School
Cutchogue, NY

Kathleen Swift, High School English Teacher
Newtown High School
Sandy Hook, CT

Connie Walser, Consultant Teacher Grades 6–8
Bay View School
Burlington, WA

About the Authors

Lois A. Lanning, PhD, is an independent education consultant. She presents and works with districts at the international, national, and state levels in the areas of literacy and Concept-Based Curriculum design.

This book is a natural extension of her three previous best-selling books in the Corwin Press Publisher's Concept-Based collection, including *Designing a Concept-Based Curriculum for English Language Arts* (2013), by Lois A. Lanning; *Concept-Based Curriculum and Instruction for the Thinking Classroom* (2nd ed., 2017), by H. Lynn Erickson, Lois A. Lanning, and Rachel French; and *Transitioning to Concept-Based Curriculum and Instruction* (2014), by H. Lynn Erickson and Lois A. Lanning.

In addition, Lois is the author of the bestselling book, *Four Powerful Strategies for Struggling Readers, Grades 3-8: Small Group Instruction That Improves Comprehension,* a joint publication between Corwin Press and the International Reading Association (2009), and a chapter in *The Best of Corwin: Differentiated Instruction in Literacy, Math, and Science* (2011), Leslie Laud, Editor.

Lois was a classroom teacher, K–12 reading consultant, special education teacher, elementary school principal, district curriculum director, adjunct professor, and finally, an assistant superintendent of schools for the last 12 years of her career in public schools. Lois is the recipient of numerous educational awards and recognitions.

Her hobbies include reading, biking, hiking, and traveling. Lois currently lives in Massachusetts with her husband. She has two children and two grandsons, whom she absolutely adores.

Tiffanee Brown, MS SpEd, is an educational consultant, National Board Certified English language arts teacher, and a teacher-leader in her school district. As an independent Dr. H. Lynn Erickson and Dr. Lois A. Lanning Concept-Based Curriculum and Instruction Presenter and Trainer, she presents and works with districts at both the regional and international levels.

Through her current position as an Instructional Design Consultant Teacher on the Teaching and Learning Team for Burlington-Edison School District in Washington State, Tiffanee leads the development of the district's Concept-Based Curriculum in science, social studies, and English language arts; supports K-12 equity focused learning design and literacy across the district; and facilitates the new teacher induction program.

Dr. Lois A. Lanning's *Designing a Concept-Based Curriculum for English Language Arts* (2013, Corwin) forever changed Tiffanee's perspective on teaching and learning, and set her passion for transforming literacy instruction in motion. She is thrilled to be the coauthor of this book to support other teachers as they strive to engage the hearts and minds of students. Tiffanee has contributed examples and resources to several recent books published by Corwin, including *Concept-Based Curriculum and Instruction for the Thinking Classroom,* 2nd ed. (Erickson, Lanning, & French, 2017), *Concept-Based Inquiry in Action* (Marschall & French, 2018), and *Measuring Human Return: Understand and Assess What Really Matters for Deeper Learning* (McEachen & Kane, 2018).

Before transitioning to her current position, Tiffanee taught English language arts, social studies, and various other classes at the middle and high school levels.

Tiffanee and her husband currently live in Washington with their two very active children. When she is not taking her kids to soccer tournaments or basketball games, she enjoys reading, gardening, snow skiing, and traveling.

E-mail: tiffaneebrown01@gmail.com

Website: www.tiffaneebrown.com

Introduction

Have you ever left a professional development workshop, or reviewed a new literacy resource, excited about the ideas, only to return to the classroom and say, "Now how do I do this?"

Both authors have had this frustrating experience. Hence, our commitment to moving Concept-Based Curriculum, and, more specifically, the 2013 book, *Designing Concept-Based Curriculum for English Language Arts* (Lanning), from curriculum units to classroom instruction. Teachers who are enthusiastic about Concept-Based Curriculum have requested resources to help support their lesson planning. Too often a well-designed, conceptual curriculum does not translate to conceptual teaching. Old habits die hard, and the transition takes some time, patience, thinking, and understanding.

This book adds another title to Corwin's Concept-Based Curriculum and Instruction series. It is a book that appeals to one's intellect and expertise, rather than one's ability to follow a script in a teaching manual. It is a practical guide for Grades 4–10 literacy teachers in the design of lessons that systematically support the transfer of students' conceptual understandings. It is a book that shares model lessons; it is also a teaching tool so that readers can transfer what they learn to their day-to-day practice.

The tenets of Erickson's original work with Concept-Based Curriculum and Instruction (CBCI) remain solid. Over the past twenty-two years, however, aspects of early thinking were tweaked, and then expanded with Lanning's contributions, and continued to be refined based on emerging cognitive research and on the feedback of hundreds of teachers around the globe who joined all of us in the Concept-Based journey.

Why this book? While many literacy resources mention that deep learning and transfer are the end goals of instruction, many of the literacy resources on the market do not actually show teachers *how* to design lessons to systematically support the transfer of students' conceptual understandings. What separates Concept-Based Curriculum and Instruction (CBCI) from other approaches is that teachers use clear, important, transferable conceptual understandings (generalizations) as specific targets of instruction and guide students to construct these understandings on their own. Generalizations give relevance to skills and support the retention and ownership of learning.

Chapter 1 begins by making a case for a strong Concept-Based Curriculum as the foundation for maximizing student learning in a literacy classroom. Some of the key points from the 2013 book, *Designing a Concept-Based Curriculum for English Language Arts* (Lanning), are referenced as a place to learn more about the complete curriculum unit design process. This chapter serves as a brief reminder/review of the components of a Concept-Based English

Curriculum unit, and includes a model literacy unit. Finally, Chapter 1 sets up the remainder of the book, which focuses on literacy teaching and learning in a Concept-Based classroom.

Chapter 2 guides teachers through the actual step-by-step process of writing Concept-Based literacy lesson plans. There is a flowchart with questions to guide your thinking and help you stay on the path to writing a quality, Concept-Based literacy lesson. A scenario between two colleagues puts the flowchart in action followed by a completed lesson plan.

Chapter 3 has many layers. First, there is a discussion of how inquiry fits naturally with Concept-Based Instruction, and how inquiry and explicit skill instruction work together in a literacy classroom. Next, there are four model literacy lesson plans, ranging from Grades 4–10. Why four? There are four strands that represent well-balanced, comprehensive literacy teaching and learning (Lanning, 2013), and each model lesson shows how to target a generalization from one strand while integrating the others. The Concept-Based Curriculum instructional units, included in the Resources section at the back of the book, show the source of each lesson plan.

This chapter also inserts "cut-out" boxes, with pertinent questions sprinkled throughout each model lesson, to guide your thinking and provoke collegial conversations. Some "cut-out" boxes describe the impact the instructional changes will have on students. These descriptions will help you know what to look for as students move their literacy learning beyond skills to conceptual understandings.

Finally, end-of-lesson reflections, followed by tables showing a progression of generalizations across grade bands, wrap up this chapter. The goal of showing generalization progressions is to illustrate the importance of keeping "the whole" or bigger picture in mind when planning students' learning experiences. The gradual and systematic inclusion of more microconcepts in upcoming generalizations ensures students are developing conceptual depth and expertise in a subject over the course of their schooling.

What does your current literacy instruction look like? Chapter 4 includes many familiar literacy practices that serve as valuable tools for Concept-Based lesson planning. There is no need or expectation to throw out all your current instruction to teach to conceptual understanding! Many known, high-impact approaches become more powerful when used as means to help students reach learning targets that stretch beyond knowledge and skills to conceptual understandings. This chapter includes many Snapshots of Concept-Based literacy classrooms showcasing learning experiences designed to deliberately cultivate students' conceptual minds and support the transfer of understanding. The different Snapshots illustrate how we engage synergistic thinking, support the process of inquiry, and help students move from a concrete skill or example to a deeper conceptual understanding about the reading, writing, speaking, and listening processes. We hope these Snapshots paint vivid pictures of Concept-Based literacy classrooms and are worth well over a thousand words!

Teachers across all our audiences, worldwide, tend to ask many of the same questions we asked when first learning about Concept-Based. Chapter 5 addresses some of these important questions as well as those we anticipate readers might be asking. These are questions such as "How does Concept-Based fit the needs of diverse learners?" "Isn't mastering the skills in standards enough?" and others. Expanding our conversations about how literacy instruction can be redesigned to become more conceptual and engaging produces student learning that is more deeply understood and enduring. Concept-Based Curriculum and Instruction continues to evolve and to become increasingly significant as a building block in teaching and learning so that all students experience the joy and empowerment associated with lifelong literacy.

CHAPTER 1

Curriculum Is the Foundation

FIGURE 1.1

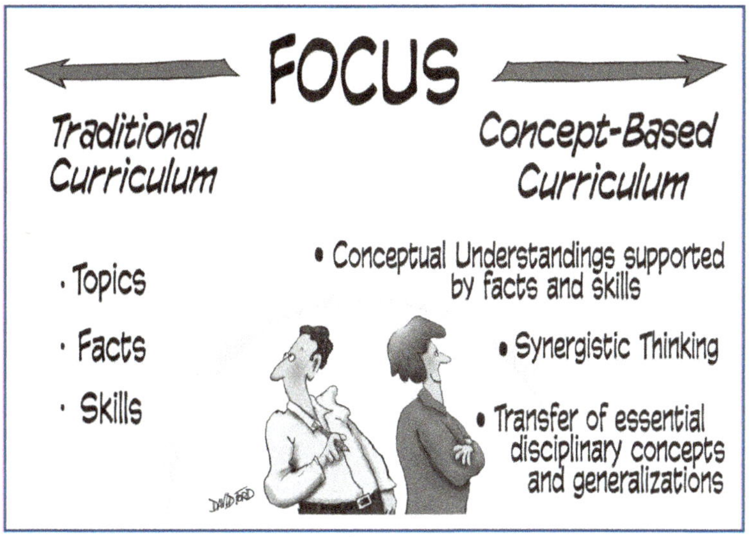

Think about how you feel when fully immersed in a good book, when you are in writing flow, or when you sense listeners hanging onto every word as you share a story. We want our students to wholeheartedly embrace their literacy learning so they, too, know what it feels like to be capable and confident readers, writers, presenters, thinkers, and discussion partners. Both authors (Lois and Tiffanee) think the *design* of a literacy lesson is how we can put students on a path toward gratifying success. We need high-quality, conceptual lessons that provoke thinking, facilitate inquiry, keep students engaged, and, ultimately, result in deep, transferable literacy learning. This book is about how to do that.

This chapter gives some background knowledge about Concept-Based Curriculum before we move into the primary purpose of this book, which is to teach the specifics of Concept-Based literacy lesson planning. The WHAT, WHY, and HOW of Concept-Based Curriculum and Instruction (CBCI) will be a review for readers familiar with CBCI. If you are new to CBCI, please know that much more in-depth information about designing curriculum units is provided in other resources written for that purpose and will help you see how this book is the logical next step. But, before we share some of the basics about Concept-Based, we begin with a quick discussion about the importance of a system-wide curriculum.

Maximizing Learning Through a Coherent Curriculum

A district-wide, Concept-Based Curriculum, comprising units of study, is the critical first step that precedes lesson planning. The book *Designing a Concept-Based Curriculum for English Language Arts* (Lanning, 2013) makes a case for curriculum serving as the master plan for improving teaching and learning. The book also extends the original Concept-Based Curriculum and Instruction (CBCI) work, developed by our dear friend and mentor, Dr. H. Lynn Erickson, by analyzing and adding the components of Concept-Based to process-oriented disciplines (English language arts, world language, fine arts, and music). Let's review a few of the key points from the 2013 book that address why curriculum design needs to come before thinking about lesson planning.

First, the definition of "curriculum" needs clarification because the term is often treated differently. Some educators refer to state or national standards as "the curriculum." Others say, "We use the expectations in our required assessments as our curriculum." Sometimes educators consider textbooks and programs by various companies and publishers as "the curriculum." On a daily basis, marketers and the Internet flood us with ads about quick, easy, ready-to-use "curricula" with a variety of promises. All these different references to "curriculum" breed confusion!

We characterize a Concept-Based Curriculum as the system-wide defined course of study, comprising approximately 4–8 instructional units across a school year, which teachers use to design lessons in the subject(s) they teach. A quality, district-wide curriculum articulates student learning targets by grade level and discipline. The curriculum also offers suggestions for designing learning experiences, timelines for rolling out each unit, ideas for differentiation, assessments to help monitor student progress, and resources available to support instruction. When teachers do not have an inclusive, viable, relevant curriculum to inform and guide their work, their jobs become even more stressful, demanding, and unclear. Left to their own devices, it is no wonder hardworking teachers often turn to textbooks, the Internet, software programs, or other prepackaged lessons and use their best judgment as to whether these resources will help their students meet standards. Acute differences among teachers' daily lesson plans mean students receive uneven experiences across classrooms, grade levels, and schools within the same system. As students move from one grade or course to the next, the disparities become more problematic. In this scenario, the lack of quality, coherent curriculum results in lower-than-expected student performance on standardized tests, even though teachers and students put in significant effort.

Students also benefit from a defined curriculum. As research indicates, students of all ages are likely to learn when their experiences connect and build on one another (Bransford, Brown, & Cocking, 1999). In other words, when learning experiences are disconnected, it is not easy to realize growth. Coherent lessons help students see the bigger whole, which fuels motivation and engagement.

A "master" curriculum creates a ripple effect. Assessments and instruction, aligned with the curriculum, better inform decisions about appropriate resources, student interventions, and professional development needs. Creating strong coherence through a system-wide curriculum should not be translated to mean there are regimented lessons where every teacher is on the same page on the same day at the same time. There needs to be flexibility in the curriculum units while still following a collective road map. An overly prescriptive curriculum forces all teachers to be clones of each other. We don't want that. But a sustained, coherent focus is lost if the curriculum is too loose or vague about expectations.

WHAT Is Concept-Based Curriculum?

There are two Structures that complement each other and graphically represent the critical components of CBCI. In Figure 1.2, the Structure of Knowledge shows how content-heavy disciplines are structured. The Structure of Process shows how process-heavy disciplines are structured. Definitions of each component of the Structures are in the sidebars. We read the graphics from the bottom up.

All subjects are made up of both disciplinary content and processes, but one Structure reflects different disciplines more than the other. For example, social studies, science, and economics are primarily structured by content (Structure of Knowledge) because there is so much subject matter knowledge to be learned. Subjects such as English, world languages, the fine arts, and music are organized primarily by processes/strategies/skills (Structure of Process). You can see this distinction by reading the state or national standards for each of these subjects. The standards for process-heavy disciplines almost always begin with a verb. Standards in process disciplines do not emphasize the content to be taught; rather they articulate *what students need to be able to* ***do***: to construct meaning; to generate a response; to critique what is viewed, read, or heard; and to produce text (print or nonprint) or a piece of music or art.

The expectation in CBCI is that students will not only learn facts and skills but take learning another step and be able to construct generalizations (conceptual understandings) that transfer. When looking over the 5–9 generalizations in a curriculum unit of instruction, you may find some of the generalizations represent essential conceptual understandings of the content under study (Structure of Knowledge). For example: *Family, friends, and community help shape a person's cultural identity* may be a central understanding drawn from the unit topic (title) or from texts used in the unit. Other generalizations in this same unit may represent essential understandings about processes (Structure of Process). For example: *Readers make inferences about people and characters using background knowledge and text evidence.* Depending on the subject, the majority of unit generalizations will be either process or knowledge.

In keeping with the integrity of the discipline, most, if not all, of the generalizations found in a literacy curriculum unit will represent important understandings about a process, strategy, or skill.

As we move teaching and learning from the bottom of the Structures up to the Generalization level, we move student thinking and learning from a lower level (facts and skills) to a higher level (conceptual understandings). Learning transfers at the conceptual level. Deeper understanding and transfer are the goals of Concept-Based Curriculum and Instruction. The curriculum and the lessons written from them are designed to deliberately and systematically develop students' intellect and conceptual minds. We don't assume engaging instructional strategies will yield this outcome.

FIGURE 1.2 THE STRUCTURE OF KNOWLEDGE AND THE STRUCTURE OF PROCESS

A Theory is a supposition or set of conceptual ideas used to explain a phenomenon or practice.

A Principle is a generalization that is considered a foundational truth for a discipline and does not use a qualifier.

A Generalization is a statement of the relationship between two or more concepts. The statement may require a qualifier. Generalizations transfer across time, cultures, and situations. Facts support generalizations.

Concepts are mental constructs drawn from a topic. Concepts are 1 or 2 words or a small phrase. Concepts are timeless, universal, abstract to different degrees and transfer.

A Topic frames the facts and is locked in time, place or situation. Topics do not transfer.

Facts provide support for Principles and Generalizations. Facts are locked in time place and situation and do not transfer.

Structure of Knowledge
Erickson, © 1995

Structure of Process
Lanning, © 2012

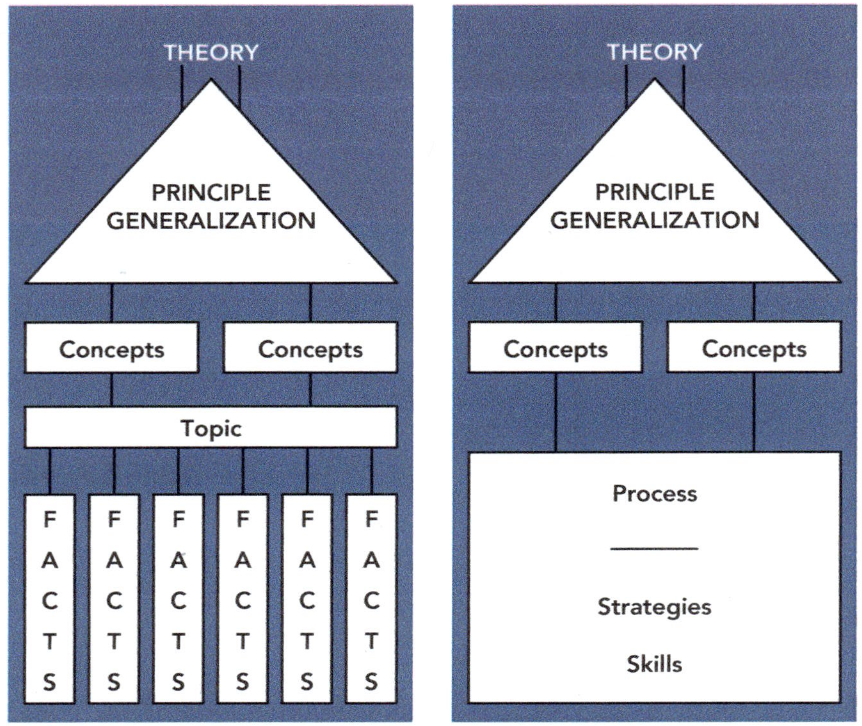

A Theory is a supposition or set of conceptual ideas used to explain a phenomenon or practice.

A Principle is a generalization that is considered a foundational truth for a discipline and does not use a qualifier.

A Generalization is a statement of the relationship between two or more concepts. The statement may include a qualifier. Generalizations transfer across time, cultures, and situations and are supported by evidence.

Concepts are mental constructs drawn from a Process, Strategy, or Skill. Concepts are 1 or 2 words or a small phrase. Concepts are timeless, universal, abstract to different degrees and transfer.

A Process is an action that produces a result and moves through stages.

Strategies are systematic plans that learners adapt and monitor to support and achieve the intended result.

Skills are the smaller operations or actions that "allow" the more complex strategies to work.

What Are the Differences Between a Concept-Based Curriculum and a More Traditional Curriculum Design?

A Concept-Based Curriculum departs from traditional curriculum designs that are based primarily on topics, facts, and skills. Concept-Based Curriculum goes beyond, because it includes a focus on the *transfer* of the essential *conceptual understandings* of a discipline and facilitates *synergistic thinking*. Here are definitions of these three important terms:

Transfer means students can apply what they learn to new situations. When learning is *understood* (versus merely memorized), one can make connections and applications to novel situations that are somewhat different (or far) from the initial experience. Perkins and Salomon (1988) distinguish *far* transfer from *near* transfer. Near transfer also requires prerequisite understanding but describes learning applied to a new situation that more closely resembles the original learning. (See Lanning, 2009, for more about transfer.)

Conceptual Understandings is another term for Generalizations. Concepts are mental constructs (ideas) that frame a set of examples sharing common attributes. **Concepts** are timeless, universal, and abstract to varying degrees (Erickson, 2008). **Generalizations** are defined as two or more concepts stated in a sentence of relationship, using a strong verb. A conceptual understanding transfers across cultures, time, and situations. For example, *The setting of a mystery supports the plot and provides the context for suspense.*

Synergistic Thinking: Erickson (2008) defines synergistic thinking as the interactive energy that occurs between the lower- and higher-order processing centers of the brain. CBCI is deliberately planned to create a "synergy" between the lower levels of thinking (facts and skills) and the higher levels of thinking (concepts and generalizations) to develop the intellect and increase motivation for learning.

These are just some of the attributes that distinguish Concept-Based Curriculum from other designs. "A Concept-Based curriculum raises the bar for curriculum, instruction, and assessment" (Erickson, 2008, p. 28). In other words, when key concepts (ideas) and generalizations of a discipline become the "drivers" for learning, we lead students to deeper understandings that transfer across different and more novel situations. Foundational skills and critical content knowledge (facts) are still important components of a Concept-Based Curriculum; however, the inclusion of conceptual understanding leverages student thinking and facilitates the retention of learning by requiring a deeper level of mental processing.

A word of caution: Merely providing teachers with a list of transferable understandings does not directly translate to a quality Concept-Based Curriculum either. If only life was so simple! Each curriculum component contributes to the coherent "whole" that articulates what students need to Know, Understand, and be able to Do. There are multiple layers in the process of writing Concept-Based units of instruction. This is why writing in teams makes so much sense. Solo writers are denied the insights and contributions of others, and the end product often reflects this disadvantage. The bottom line is that a well-designed curriculum does directly impact student performance results.

Table 1.1 serves as a quick review of the components of a Concept-Based Curriculum unit. It also summarizes some of the characteristics between a Concept-Based versus a more traditional curriculum unit. You may want to reference this chart to make better sense of the five model Concept-Based Curriculum units found in Resource A.

TABLE 1.1 COMPONENTS OF A MORE TRADITIONAL VERSUS CONCEPT-BASED LITERACY CURRICULUM UNIT

Concept-Based Curriculum Unit Components	Traditional Curriculum Unit	Concept-Based Curriculum Unit With Definitions of Each Component
1. Unit Overview	Typically, this is a brief description telling students what they will be *doing* throughout the unit.	The unit overview is written after all the other components are completed. The overview is a way a teacher can launch the unit with students using common language. Often conceptual questions are used in the unit overview to pique students' interest and activate synergistic thinking.
2. Unit Title	Names what the unit will be about. Sometimes the title is simply a bundle of skills lacking content (e.g., Grammar).	The unit title expresses what the unit will be about. It is engaging for students, yet clear about the content that will be taught. It may be written as a topic or in the form of a generative, interesting question (e.g., *Who Done It? Exploring How Mysteries Keep Us Guessing!* or *Authors as Writing Mentors*).
3. Conceptual Lens	There is no conceptual lens.	A conceptual lens is a broad (or macro) concept that provides a conceptual focus for the instructional unit and ignites synergistic thinking (as previously defined).
4. Web Strands	There are no web strands.	The web strands are predefined in a Concept-Based Literacy (process) unit. They are Understanding, Responding, Critiquing, and Producing. They represent the important dimensions of learning a process and help ensure the unit as a whole will represent comprehensive, well-balanced literacy learning. (More to come about strands.)
5. Unit Web	There is no unit web.	A unit web is an essential pre-writing tool. The unit title is written in the center with the web strands branching out like spokes on a wheel. Beneath each strand, curriculum writers brainstorm the important *concepts* and *content* that may be included in the unit.
6. Generalizations	Generalizations are usually not identified. Or there may be one "big idea" or essential question for the unit.	Generalizations identify what students are expected to Understand by the end of the curriculum unit. A unit may have 5–9 generalizations. One generalization is typically tied to the conceptual lens, and the others are derived from each web strand to ensure that all the essential dimensions of a process are addressed. Generalizations are written to very specific Concept-Based criteria. Since they represent the significant, conceptual ideas that students must *understand* as a result of the instructional unit, they move learning expectations beyond the traditional two dimensions (knowledge and skills) to a third (conceptual) dimension. Generalizations may be a statement of conceptual understanding about a process/strategy/skill or about the content under investigation. In a literacy curriculum, the majority of generalizations will be about processes since that is the nature of the discipline. Concept-Based teachers never "tell" students the generalizations. Rather they help students construct the generalizations on their own through the design of the students' learning experiences and through the use of guiding questions.

7. **Guiding Questions**	Questions tend to be fact-based and directly about the book being read or the issue under study.	There are three types of questions in a Concept-Based unit: *Factual questions* are locked in time, place, or situation and lay the foundation for learning. *Conceptual questions* transfer across examples and move students' thinking to the conceptual level. *Debatable questions* keep learning interesting by encouraging opposing viewpoints. From three to five factual and conceptual questions are written for each of the unit generalizations. Over the course of the entire unit, there may be from one to three debatable questions—depending on time. Teachers use guiding questions to draw the generalizations from students.
8. **Critical Content**	The unit includes the critical content (knowledge) students are expected to learn.	Critical content (knowledge) identifies what students are expected to Know within the curriculum unit of study. It is a bulleted list, indicating the factual content knowledge to be learned.
9. **Key Skills**	The unit includes the skills students are expected to be able to demonstrate. The skills are drawn directly from state or national standards.	Key skills list what students are expected to be able to demonstrate or Do by the end of the unit. The skills are drawn directly from state or national standards.
10. **Learning Experiences**	Most of the learning experiences within the unit ask students to read, explain, discuss, write. Standards are often driving the learning experiences. Learning experiences may be engaging, but they are not linked to a target generalization.	In this section of the instructional unit, different learning experiences are suggested (this term may be referred to as the task, activities, or assigned student work). Concept-Based learning experiences are "chunked out" in order to prepare students for the expectations of the culminating assessment task and are linked to the unit learning targets (Know, Understand, and Able to Do). A timeline, with learning experiences (directly tied to targeted unit generalizations), assessment ideas, differentiation strategies, and unit resources, are included so that teachers have a collective, clear curriculum unit road map from which to design lessons. This section of the curriculum unit should not be overly prescriptive but should offer insights into Concept-Based teaching and learning. Learning experiences need to reflect high-yield tasks that will leverage literacy learning and conceptual understanding.
11. **Culminating Assessment Task and Scoring Guide or Rubric**	The culminating assessment focuses on factual knowledge and skill proficiency. For example, in a Short Story curriculum unit, the final assessment may be to write a short story. Sometimes a common scoring tool is included but does not include an assessment of *understanding*.	A "What/Why/How" formula (Erickson, 2008) is used to design a culminating assessment task that requires students to demonstrate their *Knowledge, Skill proficiency,* as well as their *Understanding* (realization of a target generalization from the curriculum unit). The "What" and "Why" are written for teachers; the "How" is written for students. A scoring guide provides common criteria for teachers to use to evaluate the quality of the students' work/performance. The scoring tool captures what students Know, Understand, and are able to Do (skills).

WHY Concept-Based Curriculum and Instruction?

When we see the transformation that takes place in CBCI classrooms, we get excited! Here are a few answers to the question, WHY Concept-Based?

Because Concept-Based . . .

- develops structures in the brain (brain schema) for sorting, organizing, and patterning incoming information, and for transferring knowledge and skills through to the conceptual level.
- requires students to process facts and skills at a deeper intellectual level as they relate them to significant concepts, generalizations, and principles.
- engages and develops the intellect on two levels—factual/skill and conceptual.
- supports "synergistic thinking"—the cognitive interplay between the factual/skill and conceptual levels of knowledge and understanding.
- increases motivation for learning by engaging the personal intellect.
- increases fluency with language as students explain and support their deeper understandings with evidence.

The tenets of Concept-Based Curriculum and Instruction are supported by teaching and learning research, which is another reason why CBCI is important. One researcher, John Hattie, professor of education and director of the Melbourne Education Research Institute at the University of Melbourne, Australia, opened the eyes of many educators in 2009. In his book, *Visible Learning: A Synthesis of Over 800 Meta-analyses Relating to Achievement*, Hattie rank-ordered a list of influences on student learning according to their impact (effect size). Since this publication, Hattie has continued to add new factors to his meta-analyses database as the research continues to evolve. His data show that not all efforts to improve student performance yield equal results, and that in fact, some widespread practices are a waste of time, because their impact is so low. On January 18, 2017, in the electronic newsletter of The Australian Society for Evidence Based Teaching, Shaun Killian provided an update to Hattie's Effect Size list (see evidencebasedteaching.org.au). The article highlights six "super factors" that have such a strong and important effect size on student learning that it separates them from other factors. These six factors are so strong, in fact, that to include them in Hattie's overall list would skew the ratings of all the other factors. Number 5 on the "super factors" list is *Curriculum* (which is the source of this learning influence), and the curriculum factor is *Conceptual Change Programs*.

In Concept-Based Curriculum and Instruction, students' conceptual understanding is not left to chance. By deliberately specifying the generalizations students are expected to realize, teachers have clear learning targets that go beyond those for knowledge and skills. Next, by designing learning experiences and assessments that require students to demonstrate and articulate these specific conceptual understandings, misconceptions are flushed out and addressed. The impact is significant!

In 2016, Douglas Fisher and Nancy Frey joined John Hattie to apply his research specifically to literacy practices. We (Lois and Tiffanee) love the work of Fisher and Frey because teaching children to become lifelong readers and writers is our shared passion! In upcoming chapters, you will see how we integrate some of the approaches advocated by Fisher, Frey, and Hattie in *Visible Learning for Literacy* (2016) with the tenets of Concept-Based Curriculum and Instruction (CBCI).

HOW Are Concept-Based Curriculum Units of Instruction Designed?

The comprehensive answer to this question actually lies with other Concept-Based resources. Books in Corwin's Concept-Based series provide the details of writing quality Concept-Based Curriculum units. We hope you will familiarize yourself with these books to gain a deeper understanding of the design process and of the rationale for each step of curriculum writing. In this book, we define some of the curriculum unit terminology, but do not repeat all the information. Chapter 2 launches your in-depth journey in designing Concept-Based literacy lessons.

The Classroom Setting

Before we move on, however, let's think about some of the attributes of a robust literacy classroom that set the stage for Concept-Based literacy learning. We know from our collective experiences that the classroom setting in which the curriculum is taught can substantially leverage students' literacy learning. Here are our personal top four picks of requisites for every literacy classroom:

- **Use authentic, quality literacy resources and tasks.** When students read diverse texts representing the richness of natural language, they are exposed to a wealth of vocabulary, ideas across different contexts, and unique forms of expression. Students come to appreciate the dexterity of language. Most literacy teachers readily agree that authentic and diverse texts, materials, and tasks are beneficial to the language-learning process.
- **Blend direct/explicit instruction along with guided practice and inquiry.** There are times when processes need to be explicitly taught. See: *Four Powerful Comprehension Strategies for Struggling Readers* (Lanning, 2009), and *Reading Reasons: Motivational Mini Lessons for Middle and High School* (Gallagher, 2003). A critical goal in a Concept-Based classroom is also to provide more opportunities for student inquiry. We want students to examine and analyze concepts across different situations and examples, so they can construct an understanding based on their synthesis of the idea represented. To support students' construction of their understanding (generalization) requires an appropriate blend of explicit and inquiry instructional approaches.
- **Create a literacy rich environment.** Learning how language works means accessing and using language frequently. A classroom filled with books, walls covered with examples of students' writing, desk or chair arrangements that encourage small group discussions and collaborative work, a culture where risk-taking is valued—these are just some of the ways to create a welcoming and motivating literacy community.
- **Provide student choice.** When students have opportunities to make choices about the texts they will read, the products they will produce, the learning goals to work toward, and the topics they wish to write about, they have greater ownership of school assignments and higher intrinsic motivation to do the work. We aren't talking about carte blanche classroom choice; we are talking about looking for ways that allow students to be involved in decisions that will empower and inspire them as learners.

The classroom sets the stage for literacy instruction. And a classroom setting, just as the setting of a story, "can help set the mood, influence the way characters behave, affect the dialog, foreshadow events, invoke an emotional response, reflect the society in which the characters live, and sometimes even plays a part in the story." (https://thewritingplace.wordpress.com/2010/04/13/story-elements-importance-of-the-setting/)

Summary

We are now ready to dig into Concept-Based lesson design. Chapter 2 provides a step-by-step explanation and rationale to get you started on your journey to becoming a master Concept-Based teacher. We will show you how being deliberate and knowledgeable in lesson planning can support the development of students' intellect and their conceptual minds.

Extending Thought

1. What are some of the consequences of teachers across a system (school or district) not having common units of instruction?
2. Why do you think students often do not retain what they learn year to year? Why do you think students struggle transferring their learning to new situations?
3. How do you see the design of Concept-Based Curriculum and Instruction addressing the concerns expressed in questions 1 and 2?
4. Do you see yourself as a Concept-Based teacher? Why or why not?

CHAPTER 2

Designing Concept-Based Literacy Lessons

FIGURE 2.1

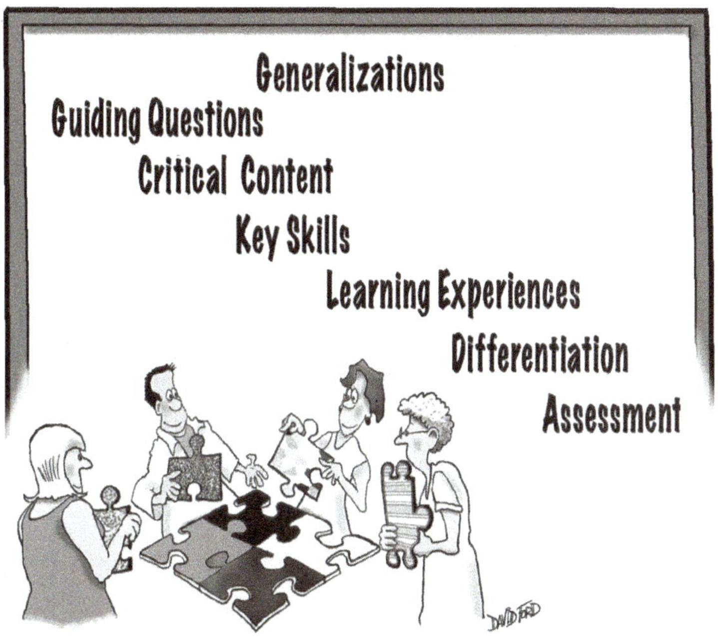

Designing Learning for Conceptual Understanding and Transfer

Moving Concept-Based instructional units into classroom practice is where the rubber hits the road. It is also where our best intentions run the highest risk of falling apart! Reverting to familiar ways is natural.

Both authors know the time we spent as teachers each Sunday planning instruction for the coming week. The steps in writing a CBCI lesson may look daunting at first glance, but with practice and collaboration, it will get easier. The goal is to help you think about and plan the conceptual aspects of a lesson ahead of delivery. Many factors affect the success of instruction; however, inappropriate or haphazard planning is the number one reason Concept-Based

Instruction falters. Lesson planning is more efficient when multiple minds work together. We know teacher isolation is the enemy of progress (Erickson & Lanning, 2014), so we highly encourage collaboration.

Concept-Based Literacy Lessons

Lesson plans are not foolproof. But writing out the critical elements of instruction clarifies thinking, serves as a reference for future planning, creates a document for collaboration, and reflects your dedication to quality teaching. A Concept-Based lesson plan charts a deliberate path to students' conceptual understanding. The more that goes into thinking through a lesson, the higher the chances are the execution of the plan will go smoothly, and the learning targets will be met.

There needs to be coherence among the components of a Concept-Based lesson. This means:

1. the factual content and skills exemplify or build the necessary foundational knowledge about the generalization students are expected to realize,
2. guiding questions are appropriately used to bridge students' thinking from lower to higher levels of thinking required to construct the generalization,
3. the learning experiences (student work) are designed to support students' learning of the knowledge, processes, and/or generalizations under study, and finally,
4. assessments are aligned with the learning targets (knowledge, skills, and understanding) of the lesson.

Yes, there is much to consider when planning a Concept-Based lesson. The lesson planner template that follows helps structure the components, maintains the integrity of the CBCI unit, and makes planning more manageable. Again, codesigning lessons with colleagues is a proven way to expedite the process.

Let's begin to draft a Concept-Based literacy lesson using the following steps. Becoming familiar with what each step entails will help you make better sense of the resulting model lesson in Figure 2.6.

Steps in Planning a Concept-Based Literacy Lesson

Step 1: Review Your Concept-Based Literacy Curriculum Unit From Which the Lesson Is Coming

Going back and holistically looking over the curriculum unit the lesson is coming from helps create an overall picture of what instruction intends to accomplish. What if you do not have a school or district Concept-Based literacy curriculum? Starting your Concept-Based journey without an instructional unit is not ideal as it sets the stage for effective lesson planning, but until you have a written curriculum, this book will help your lessons better activate and develop your students' conceptual minds.

Note: If you compare the components of a Concept-Based lesson planner (Figure 2.2) with those in the model Concept-Based Curriculum units (found in Resource A), you will see how the components of the two align.

FIGURE 2.2 CONCEPT-BASED LESSON PLANNER

CONCEPT-BASED LESSON PLANNER

Unit Title ______________________ **Instructor** ______________________

Subject ______________________ **Grade Level** ______________________

Lesson Number ______________________ **Lesson Time Frame** ______________________

Lesson Opening: (to be communicated with students at lesson onset):

Learning Targets: What students will Understand (Generalizations), Know and be able to do (Skills)

Generalization(s) (Students will understand that . . .) Note: Generalizations may apply to one or a series of lessons

1.

Guiding Questions

1a.

1b.

etc.

Strand	**Critical Content (Know)**	**Key Skills (Able to Do)**
Understanding:		
Responding:		
Critiquing:		
Producing:		

Learning Experiences	**Differentiations**

Materials/Resources:

Assessments:

Closing:

Teacher Notes:

Step 2: Identify and Insert the Lesson Learning Targets

The lesson Learning Targets are copied and pasted directly from a written Concept-Based Curriculum unit. Again, if you do not have access to a Concept-Based Curriculum unit, you can begin changing traditional lessons into more conceptual lessons by first identifying the important understanding (generalization) you want students to realize and be able to transfer by the end of the lesson. *Designing a Concept-Based Curriculum for English Language Arts* (Lanning, 2013) guides you through the process of crafting quality generalizations.

Three Types of Lesson Learning Targets:

A. **Generalizations** are statements that express the conceptual relationship between two or more concepts. Generalizations are summaries of thought we want students to construct as a result of their learning to demonstrate conceptual understanding. The design of the learning experiences, coupled with appropriate guiding questions, will move students' thinking to a generalization.

You might be asking, "How are the unit generalizations determined?" Did you see the web in the model instructional unit, *The Art of Argumentation*, in Resource A-2? During the process of writing the unit, teachers brainstormed the concepts, strand by strand, around the web. These concepts were then used to craft Generalizations. Each curriculum unit includes a generalization related to the conceptual lens (which provides the broad, conceptual focus for the entire unit), and 1–2 generalizations for each web strand. In a process discipline, like literacy, one generalization may represent more than one strand due to the interplay among the different strands. Looking back at the definition and examples in Chapter 1, you will notice generalizations require two or more concepts written in a statement of relationship using a strong verb. Figure 2.3 depicts how two or more concepts, brainstormed while creating the curriculum unit web, are used to craft a generalization.

FIGURE 2.3 GENERALIZATION VISUAL

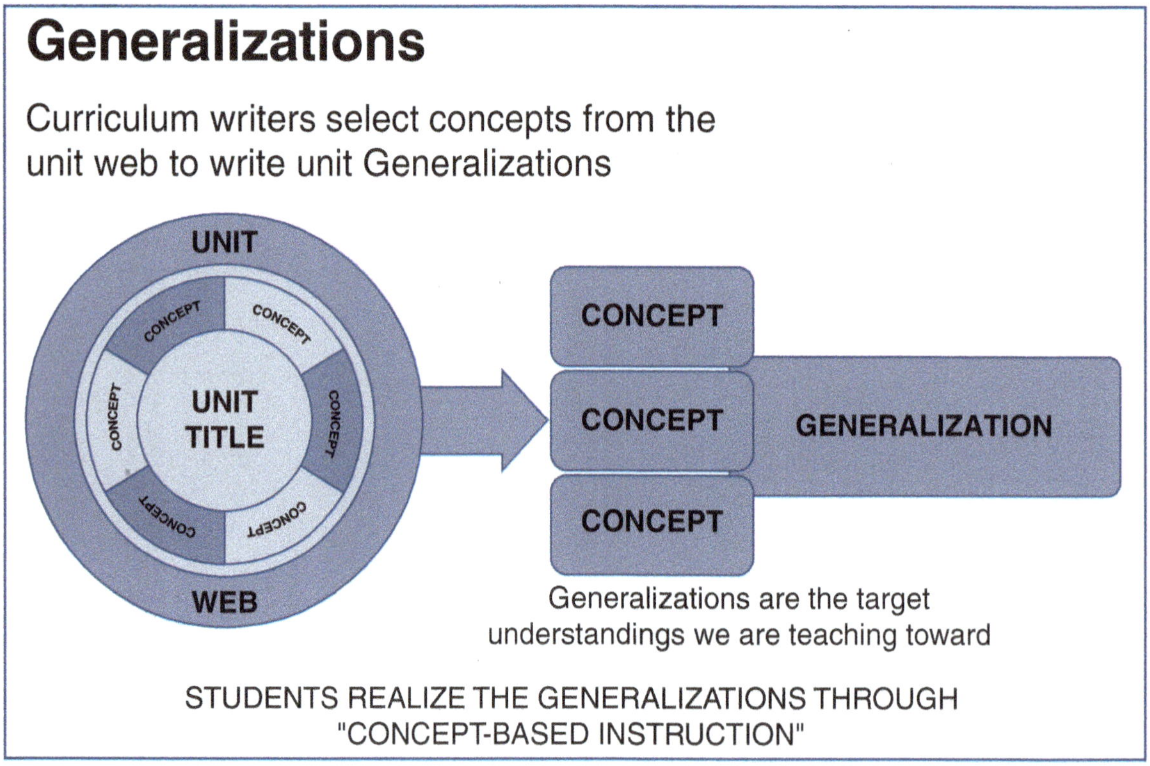

- **Note: Guiding Questions** are included in the lesson plan to help teachers direct students' thinking toward the target generalization. The guiding questions come in three types:
  - Factual questions help build the foundational knowledge students need to construct the target generalization. They focus thinking on a particular point, and the answers provide substantiation for generalizations.
  - Conceptual questions move student thinking to a higher level and help bridge a specific example to a conceptual idea. These questions ask about conceptual relationships, which forces linking, and they require more sophisticated levels of cognitive processing and thinking. Conceptual questions are transferable across multiple examples and situations.
  - Debatable questions are not in every lesson, but they are used enough throughout the unit to keep students engaged and able to take a stand on an issue that has no right or wrong answer. The answer must be defended. Debatable questions require an analysis and synthesis of different sources and perspectives.

B. **Critical Content** lists the factual knowledge students are expected to Know by the end of the lesson. (See this component in *The Art of Argumentation* Unit in Resource A-2.) It is helpful to use the stem, "Students will Know . . ." as you write the Critical Content. Otherwise, you might slip back into writing a generalization or skill.

C. **Key Skills** identify what students are expected to be able to Do (demonstrate) and are drawn directly from the disciplinary state or national standards relevant to the particular lesson. (Again, see Resource A-2.)

Organizing the Critical Content and Key Skills Learning Targets by Literacy Strand:

Strands represent the four essential aims of literacy learning—Understanding, Responding, Critiquing, and Producing (Lanning, 2013). Students need instruction and practice in each of these strands to truly understand and master a complex process.

There are two primary roles the four literacy strands play in CBCI, but first, let's define each:

- Strand 1: *Understanding* represents the knowledge, skills, or concepts that will help students construct meaning about the content material under study.
- Strand 2: *Responding* describes the knowledge, skills, or concepts students need to generate a meaningful reaction to or reflection of their learning. Responding requires students to pause, think, listen, consider other perspectives, and learn how to contribute positively to group discourse before jumping to judgment about what is heard, viewed, or read.
- Strand 3: *Critiquing* represents the knowledge, skills, or concepts needed to take a stance, to make an informed evaluation, and to support a critique with relevant evidence. Critiquing is evaluating, analyzing, and judging what is heard, viewed, and read to be better consumers of information in the world.
- Strand 4: *Producing* represents the knowledge, skills, or concepts necessary to producing a piece, either print (written text) or nonprint (for example, a presentation, a visual, and the like).

The Purpose of Strands in a Concept-Based Literacy Curriculum *Unit*:

The first way to consider the strands is by the role they play in writing a Concept-Based Literacy Unit. Strands provide the structure to ensure the CBCI Unit reflects comprehensive and well-balanced literacy teaching and learning. The strands are used in the curriculum unit in two different sections. Again, looking at the unit web in Resource A-2, you will see how we first draw out the ideas (concepts) relevant to the unit according to each literacy strand. These concepts are then used to help write robust unit generalizations, strand by strand.

When you look at the unit generalizations in Resource A-2, do you see how each generalization reflects an important understanding about one or more of the four process strands? Sometimes a process-based curriculum unit will include one or two Structure of Knowledge generalizations, which represent important conceptual understandings about the *content* under study (for example, a theme statement that cuts across a collection of texts or an essential understanding about a topic). Be cautious, however, not to let more than a couple of the unit generalizations shift the emphasis of learning to the "big ideas" about the texts. Yes, we want students to remember some of the enduring messages of literature; however, teaching literacy is more about building students' essential understandings of how language works. This means the majority of generalizations in a process-based curriculum unit, like literacy, need to reflect the important conceptual understandings we want students to realize about the processes, strategies, or skills within the unit. In other words, Structure of Process generalizations.

When you are unsure of which Structure a generalization is from, think about the instruction needed to guide students to the target understanding. For example, a generalization such as, *Mystery and suspense narratives utilize common literary devices within unique text structures*, may initially be thought of as a Structure of Knowledge generalization. However, think about the instruction students will need in order to arrive at this understanding. Students need to learn about the literary devices used in both genres, and they need to uncover how each gene is typically structured. For example, a mystery is structured by presenting the reader with a puzzle or problem up front, with the rest of the story wrestling with how to solve it, whereas suspense narratives build the tension over time. Because the teaching and learning behind this conceptual understanding focuses on literacy concepts and substantiation for the generalization does not come from what the text is about (content); rather, from analyzing and critiquing how the texts are crafted, it represents a Structure of Process generalization.

Second, within the model curriculum unit, you will see how the same four strands are used to organize the Critical Content (Knowledge) and Key Skills that students will learn by the end of the unit. If we don't flush out what we expect students to Know and be able to Do by each strand, we can easily shortchange comprehensive, well-balanced literacy teaching and learning.

The Purpose of Strands in a Concept-Based Literacy *Lesson Planner*:

The second way to consider the strands is by the role they play in writing a Concept-Based literacy lesson planner. To grow independent and proficient readers, writers, speakers, thinkers, and so on, we need to design learning experiences that address each of the four strands. In the lesson planner, usually one generalization from the curriculum unit, emphasizing a particular strand, is identified as the learning target for students *conceptual understanding*. In the same lesson plan, the learning targets, for what students will *know* (Critical Content) and be able to *do* (Key Skills) by the end of the lesson, are copied directly from each of the four strand sections in the curriculum unit. You will see in the model lesson plans ahead how the knowledge and skill learning targets span all of the four strands to ensure none of the essential strands of literacy learning is slighted as students work their way to uncovering and understanding the target generalization.

Step 3: Preparing the Lesson Opening

As in writing, a good hook introduces a lesson, captures students' attention, and sets the wheels of learning in motion. Intriguing questions that might pique students' interest or a short scenario read aloud are just a couple of options for a lesson opening. Remember, conceptual lesson plans typically extend over several classes or days. A lesson opening that gets students eager to hear more is not only a useful classroom management tool, but it also triggers conceptual thinking right from the start.

Step 4: Design the Lesson Learning Experiences and Suggest Ways to Differentiate

Now that you have a clear understanding of the learning targets and the conceptual focus of the lesson, the next step is to design learning experiences that will help students meet these targets. Learning experiences are logically sequenced and incrementally more demanding across lessons to prepare students for success on the culminating unit assessment as well as for meeting the learning targets of an individual lesson. The majority of lessons in Concept-Based represent inductive teaching using guided or structured inquiry. The learning experiences assigned to students require them to question, investigate, ponder, grapple, critically analyze, dialogue, look for patterns, and synthesize the content and skills under study. We are not saying there will never be pauses where instruction zooms in and becomes more explicit, but, for the most part, students are building their conceptual understanding through inquiry assignments coupled with the teacher's guiding questions that path thinking toward the generalization.

As you design your learning experiences, keep in mind the students who may need a greater challenge and those who may need more support. One of the many benefits of a Concept-Based approach is that it naturally supports differentiation. This is because Concept-Based is structured around the essential ideas (concepts) of a discipline. What this means is that the target generalization remains the same for all students; however, the materials and assignments leading students to the generalization may be adjusted according to students' needs. All students are capable of thinking and understanding. If instruction provides the right scaffolds, there is no need to water down the target generalization. More thoughts about differentiation in Concept-Based Instruction, for struggling as well as advanced students, are shared in the Q&A of Chapter Five.

Step 5: Assessment

Think about how you will assess your students' Knowledge, Understanding, and Skill learning targets. As teachers, we are all highly experienced in designing assessments of students' knowledge and skills. Pop quizzes, multiple-choice tests, and fill-in-the-blank types of checkups on student learning are fine—sometimes—but not if they are the only types of assessments. Assessing generalizations requires a different type of assessment. One trick we use in Concept-Based is to make sure we pick up some of the conceptual language used in the target generalization when we create an assessment of conceptual understanding. We want to head students' thinking in the right direction as they are constructing and, ultimately, articulating and defending the target generalization.

You will see from the various unit and lesson plan examples in this book that sometimes students are asked to simply write a statement of the relationship among key concepts on an

Exit Slip when they leave class. This is a highly cognitive exercise that clearly measures students' understanding. A simple and effective Exit Slip is to ask students to finish the following sentence stem, "I understand that . . ." or if students are working in collaborative teams, "We understand that . . ."

Assessments of understanding may also be more intensive and comprehensive. For example, asking students to complete a performance task that requires them to demonstrate proficiency by integrating targeted skills, knowledge of content, and conceptual understanding. A quick reminder: Scoring tools for a CBCI unit's culminating assessment (such as rubrics or other types shown in the model units) need to capture all three dimensions—what students **K**now, **U**nderstand, and can **D**o.

Step 6: Lesson Closing

The lesson closing is a good time for you and your students to collectively summarize the lesson, including reflections about process as well as product. Can students explain *why* they did what they did as a reader, writer, speaker, listener, or viewer? Teachers frequently build in time for students to share and explain their product, but they fail to ask students to explain their process. The ability to transfer learning to new and novel situations requires self-awareness and understanding of both. We don't want students simply engaged in the rote application of skills or strategies. Take a moment to think about your own unique instructional toolbox. What strategies do you currently find effective to bring closure to lessons? Chances are, with minor tweaks, they could also be used as a tool to move learning to conceptual understanding. What is most important is that we don't want to leave understanding to chance.

A variety of assessments can be found in each of the model unit and lesson examples in upcoming chapters.

Finally, the lesson closing should lay the path for learning yet to come. Helping students see how the lesson will build toward future learning strengthens relevance and connections among lessons.

Resources to Guide the Lesson-Planning Process

Figure 2.4 illustrates the three-dimensional Concept-Based literacy instruction we are striving for. Think of the illustration as a pinwheel. The modes of literacy, in the second ring, rotate. The outer section rotates, also, because all aspects of both the middle and outer sections are interrelated. Notice the components of Concept-Based literacy (captured on the outermost sections of the illustration) are relevant across all modes of literacy (reading, writing, speaking, listening, and viewing). Collectively, these components are necessary elements of instruction in each mode of literacy to ensure conceptual understanding and transfer. Process, strategy, and skill instruction did not get sidestepped. In fact, strategies and skills provide the foundation for understanding literacy, serve as catalysts for moving thinking and learning from a lower to a higher level, and provide substantiation for the target generalizations.

Writing a Concept-Based lesson plan requires a professional mind shift. CBCI teachers consistently ask, "As a result of my instruction, what is the important conceptual understanding (generalization) I want my students to understand and be able to transfer independently to new situations?" Deliberately writing the target generalization (using Concept-Based criteria to check quality) gives the lesson that essential, conceptual third dimension, which makes a difference in learning retention and transfer. Concept-Based instruction does not work well for teachers who want a script to follow or ask, "Just tell me what to do!" Cultivating

FIGURE 2.4 THREE-DIMENSIONAL, CONCEPT-BASED LITERACY

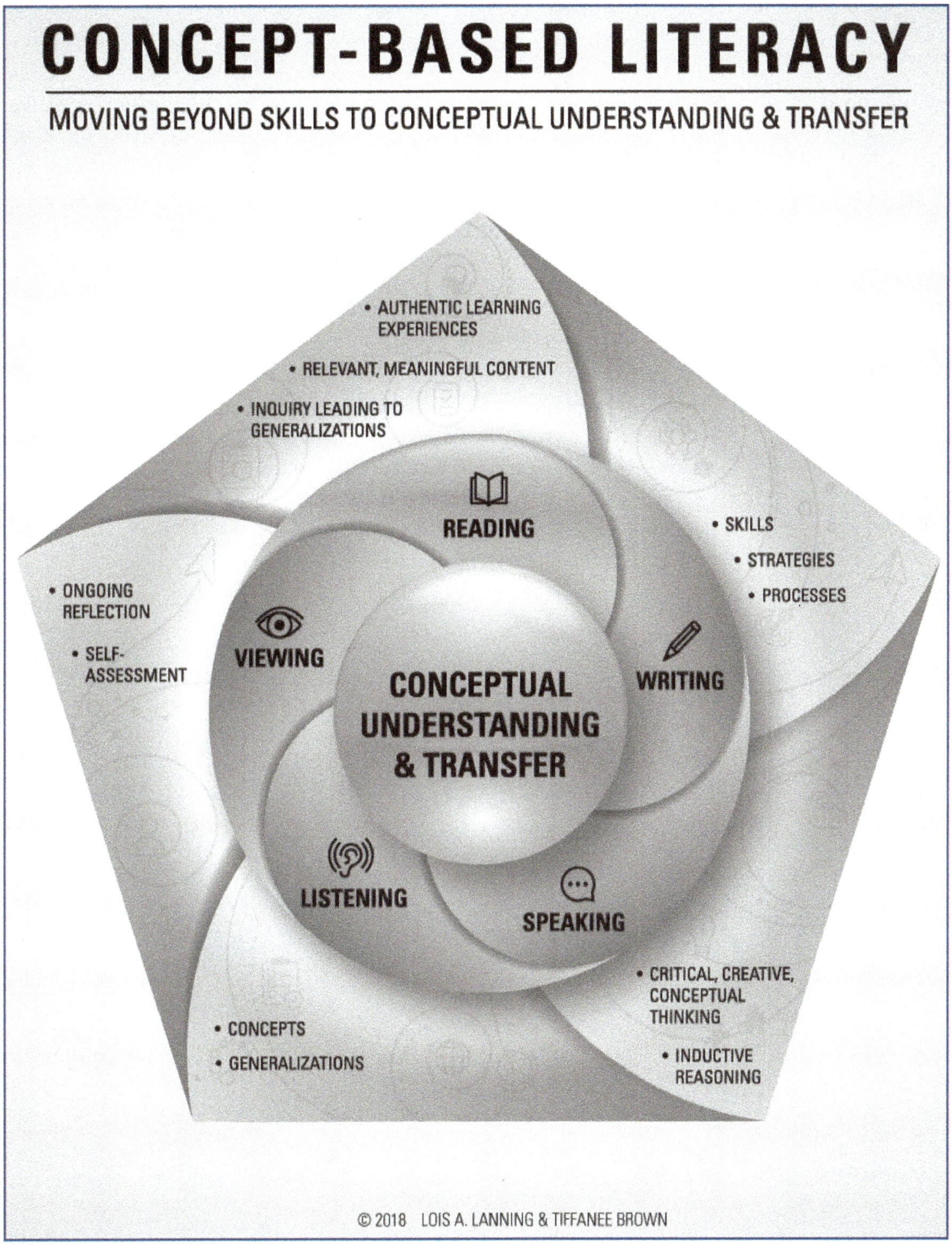

thinking students requires thinking teachers. The questions offered in the flowchart are intended to help build teacher agency—or ownership of the Concept-Based design process. The more deeply one understands the tenets of Concept-Based, the greater the influence it will have across the vast array of instructional decisions teachers continuously make. Rubrics and other tools included in this book are a way to monitor ongoing progress in becoming a CBCI teacher. It does take time; it is a learning process.

Sample Essential Generalization Criteria:

- Does the generalization represent a statement of relationship between at least two concepts joined by a strong, present tense verb?
- Does the generalization reflect a conceptual understanding that is important to the inquiry?
- Does the generalization transfer to other literacy contexts?

(See complete checklist in Erickson, Lanning, & French, 2017)

A Flowchart to Guide Thinking

The flowchart, *Thinking Through the Design of a Concept-Based Lesson*, Figure 2.5 visually depicts the process of lesson plan writing. Erickson (2008) used the terms 2D and 3D to distinguish curriculum and instruction that reflects only two dimensions—*knowledge* (topics and facts) and *skills*—versus curriculum and instruction with a third dimension added—*conceptual understanding*. In each step of the flowchart, the questions and criteria are to provoke conversations that will help ensure your lesson plan reflects a three-dimensional design and deepens your understanding of the intentions of Concept-Based Instruction.

The flowchart also aligns with the components of the Concept-Based lesson planner template. After reviewing the flowchart, you will find a scenario between two colleagues using the flowchart as a collaborative tool (Table 2.1). The scenario allows you to "hear" the thought process, the two-way conversation, and the teacher's self-reflection. If you do not have a peer collaborator, we think the flowchart and scenario will benefit your planning, too. (Helpful Hint: It may be useful to refer to the lesson planner template in Figure 2.1 as you follow this conversation.)

FIGURE 2.5 THINKING THROUGH THE DESIGN OF A CONCEPT-BASED LESSON

Thinking Through the Design of a Concept-Based Lesson

Begin by reviewing the Concept-Based Curriculum Unit on which the lesson will be based. (Note: A lesson spans several days or class sessions as it takes time, multiple examples, and guidance in order for students to uncover generalizations.)

1

Questions to Help You Begin Moving From the Curriculum Unit to the Lesson Plan Template

- **Consider the unit as a whole:**
  - *How do all the components of the unit (collectively) shape your thinking about how you might teach this unit?*
  - *How will today's lesson build on concepts and/or generalizations from previous learning?*
  - *What content is reflected in the unit title?*
  - *How does the unit's conceptual lens shape your thinking about the focus of this unit?*
- **Review the organization of the lesson plan template**

2

From the Curriculum Unit, Identify the Lesson Learning Targets

- *What do you expect students to* ***Know*** *(critical content),* ***Understand*** *(1–2 generalizations), and/or be able to* ***Do*** *(key skills) by the end of this lesson?*
- *How will you sequence the guiding questions to help maintain a focused connection with your targeted generalization? In other words, do the questions provide a logical "path" that leads students' thinking inductively toward the lesson generalization?*
- *How many days (class periods) do you anticipate it will take for students to realize the lesson's learning targets?*

3

Preparing the Lesson Opening

- How will the lesson opening engage students' minds, interests, and curiosities?
- What conceptual question or lens can be used to ignite students' synergistic thinking?

Consider the elements of a minilesson as a structure for your opening:

- **Connect** how this lesson will fit with previous learning.
- **Pose** an overarching conceptual question or introduce concepts that will be investigated in this lesson. (1–3 minutes)
- **Model & Teach** (by thinking aloud) the types of thinking and work students will be expected to demonstrate in their upcoming learning experience. Use academic and conceptual language and guiding questions to direct students' thinking. (5–10 minutes)
- Briefly **Engage** students in the learning by having them apply, or imagining themselves applying, what they were taught. (3–5 minutes)
- Create **a Link** from the minilesson to the assigned/inquiry task (1–2 minutes) and **release** students to begin their work.

4

Planning the Learning Experiences (student work, tasks, activities)

- *Which instructional techniques will best support learning in this lesson? (graphic organizer, discussion, quick write, role play, debates, and so forth.)*
- *Is any explicit instruction needed before or during the students' inquiry task?*

Think through the criteria for evaluating quality learning experiences in the checklist below:

- ☐ The learning experience reflects a gradual release model, transitioning the responsibility from teacher to student.
- ☐ The learning experiences require students to reason their way through the work—for example, the tasks necessitate students' intellectual engagement in "figuring things out," integrating thinking, and ongoing reflection and self-assessment.
- ☐ The guiding questions, paired with the texts, tasks, and/or examples students are investigating, lead to and exemplify the target generalization.
- ☐ The learning experiences help students to begin to uncover and link patterns across different examples.
- ☐ The assigned work represents an authentic, meaningful context (as much as possible) and is relevant to future learning.
- ☐ The learning experiences often require peer collaboration.
- ☐ The learning experiences are differentiated to ensure equitable access for all learners.
  - by providing multiple points of entry into the concepts under study,
  - by how students are grouped,
  - by making sure the materials (for example, text) are at an appropriate level,
  - by the complexity of the learning experience,
  - by the amount of teacher guidance and scaffolding provided, and
  - by providing opportunities for student voice and choice.

5

Assessment

- *How will you* ***assess*** *your students'* ***K****nowledge,* ***U****nderstanding, and* ***S****kills throughout the lesson and at the end?*
- *What* ***data*** *will you collect from this lesson?*
- *When students arrive at the generalization, will you post the generalization for future reference?*

6

Lesson Closing and Final Questions for Reflection

- *How will you* ***close*** *the lesson?*
- *How did the learning in this lesson connect with previous learning?*
- *How will you and the students collaboratively reflect on the learning (process and product)?*
- *How will this lesson build toward future learning?*
- *How will you* ***reinforce the transferability*** *of the generalization?*
- *How will you plan interventions for those students who are struggling or who need more challenge?*

TABLE 2.1 THE FLOWCHART IN ACTION: A COLLABORATIVE CBCI LESSON-PLANNING SCENARIO

Session 1	
Literacy Coach:	Hi, Michelle! Since your class will be starting the district's new literacy curriculum next week, this is the perfect time for us to sit together and begin planning your first CBCI lesson.
Teacher:	I am nervous about this but also excited about the possibilities! This unit sounds so much more comprehensive than the way I used to teach argumentative writing!
Literacy Coach:	Tell me; what you are most nervous about?
Teacher:	Well, I want to do this right. . . . There is so much I need to learn about how CBCI works.
Literacy Coach:	As with anything new, it will take time and practice and continued learning to build your understanding and confidence. BUT, we are in this together and will take small steps to get you more comfortable. Let's start by looking through the new Concept-Based Literacy Curriculum unit together. We want to get a good sense of the whole before we dive into crafting a lesson plan.
[The new Grade 10 CBCI Unit is titled, "*The Art of Argumentation.*"]	
Literacy Coach:	I do love the title! I know students will grab onto this right away. The conceptual lens of the unit is *argumentation*, which makes perfect sense. Remember, a conceptual lens serves as a perceptual filter under which the more microconcepts of the unit will be organized and studied. How does the unit's conceptual lens shape your thinking about the focus of this unit?
Teacher:	Well, my mind is already thinking about how I need to make sure I have a range of examples of effective arguments so that students can see how the components of an argument work together to create impact.
Literacy Coach:	Love it! You are already talking like a synergist thinker when you link a concept with specific factual examples—this is exactly how CBCI will begin deliberately developing conceptual schemas in our students' minds. Okay, now that we have skimmed through the whole unit and refreshed our understanding of terminology, let's identify the learning targets for your first lesson. In other words, what do you expect students to **K**now, be able to **D**o, and **U**nderstand by the end of this lesson?
Teacher:	I think I will make the unit's first generalization the learning target, "*The effective organization of the components of an argument advance an author's claim.*" The biggest shift in my teaching is going to be to design an inquiry that leads students to this understanding and to expect them to construct it on their own. Getting them there is what is a little scary. But, yes, I can see how the target generalization determines the foundational knowledge and skills they will need in order to get to this understanding. It means I have to really think through the activities—or learning experiences as they are called in the unit—that will help lead students to the generalization.
Literacy Coach:	Your thinking is exactly right. These are the critical elements that need to be thought through as we plan. To break this down a bit, let's first identify the fundamental concepts in the target generalization.
Teacher:	Well, the concept of *argumentation* is key here. Claim, reasons, evidence, and counterclaims are also important microconcepts.
Literacy Coach:	Yes, and the generalization also expresses *why* authors craft and organize an argument with these components. Let's hold these thoughts as we keep working. Thinking about the students in your class, how many lessons do you anticipate it will take for students to realize the target generalization?
Teacher:	I would say maybe 3–5 by the time we learn more about the components, see how they work together in texts, and why . . . and, again, I need to find the right texts.
Literacy Coach:	Articles about government policies come to my mind as you are talking. We certainly are rich in these, given the current political polarization we hear about every day! We are off to a good start. Now where do you see explicit instruction may be needed?
Teacher:	I am thinking I do need to do some explicit teaching at the start to give my students a common knowledge and skill base. I may also need to pause the inquiry to provide more explicit instruction if I see a need.
Literacy Coach:	Sounds good. Last question to end our work today: Do you think there may be opportunities for student choice in the lesson?
Teacher:	Yes, I can see opportunities for having them select topics of interest from the range of different sample texts I offer. Thanks for getting my mind going. I look forward to starting to write out the lesson.

Session 2	
Teacher:	Hi! I wanted you to see how I already started completing the CBCI lesson plan template based on our conversation yesterday. I just had to get started! I pulled out the target generalization and guiding questions I'll be using from the curriculum unit. You will see, I added a couple more guiding questions based on what I know my students will need. These will be a big help to me. I need the exact wording of the different types of questions right now to make sure I am balancing factual and conceptual and to make sure I am specifically guiding my students' thinking. Then, I pulled out the specific Critical Content and Key Skills from the curriculum unit that I will use as learning targets for the lesson. I decided I am going to be using the lesson opening as it is written in the curriculum unit, because first of all, I think it is really powerful, and it will get kids' attention right away. Second, because this is my first lesson, it launches everything beautifully.
Literacy Coach:	Fantastic. Your work really helps get us going today. I totally agree with you about having the guiding questions in writing in front of you and adding more of your own. The questions are critical in helping you monitor and guide students' thinking throughout the lesson. Let's look over the order of the ones you listed. A question I always ask is, "Do the questions follow a logical 'path' that will lead students' thinking inductively toward the generalization?" In other words, you may need to scaffold the questions—start with the factual to build students' foundational knowledge, and gradually move to the conceptual questions. Here is another thing I'd like your reaction to; you mentioned last time that you taught argumentation writing in the past. What are some of the similarities and differences between your previous lessons and this one?
Teacher:	In response to the order of the guiding questions, yes, good idea. I will definitely reflect on the sequence of my questions and probably need to be flexible while I am teaching, depending on how things go. The biggest shift I see from my former teaching is the explicit focus I am putting on concepts and on getting kids to the generalizations without telling them. Teaching the knowledge and skills of argumentation are pretty much what I have always done.
Literacy Coach:	Great! So, you aren't throwing everything out but are building that third dimension: conceptual understanding. Okay, so back to your lesson opening. I love the unit overview that is in the curriculum unit, too, but I think we might narrow it down a bit at the end. We want to tie it directly to your lesson and use the opening to activate students' synergistic thinking. Because, as we talked about yesterday, the concept of *argumentation* is key to the lesson generalization, is there a way to sharpen your opening, so you more deliberately ignite students' conceptual minds after you read aloud the curriculum unit overview?
Teacher:	Hmmm. . . . I could ask them to think of situations when they felt really compelled or convinced by an argument that they heard recently. Then they could reflect on why they think that argument resonated with them.
Literacy Coach:	I agree! I imagine they will quickly have many examples of situations with parents, school personnel, older siblings, and especially things they've heard or encountered while reading or watching the news! You could begin to capture student responses to that opening question on chart paper under three headers, "Audience," "Claim," and "Impact." I can almost hear a student saying things like, "My Mom is always claiming texting while driving kills people. She is trying to prove to me how dangerous it is so that I don't make the same mistake." You would then write "*Teen driver*" under <u>Audience,</u> and "*Texting while driving kills*" under <u>Claim,</u> and then list "*Fear changes behavior*" under the heading <u>Impact</u>. You will be creating a visual of the relationship among the concepts, with specific examples of each. Do you see how this will get them primed for the lesson? Moving on to the learning experiences section of the lesson plan template. . . . Now, is there an interesting piece of short mentor text that you might use, after you open the lesson, that exemplifies an effective organization of the components of an argument? This would help you zero in on the Critical Content learning targets you identified in your lesson plan under the section, "Students will **K**now." Let's look back at the unit planner where it indicates what students should **K**now—the components of an argument and types of evidence.
Teacher:	I need to look at some more resources, but yes, this is doable.
Literacy Coach:	As we mentioned before, we want students to investigate patterns across different examples of text, reflect, and synthesize the information, so they can ultimately construct the generalization on their own. This is why using short texts, which illustrate your learning targets, work so well. It keeps our "teacher talk time" to the point, gives students an opportunity to share what they are getting out of your example, and allows increasingly more time for them to apply what they are learning, together or individually. This represents a gradual release of responsibility. I know you've used a minilesson format in some of your writing classes previously. The structure of a minilesson works perfectly here. By listening to you think aloud in the minilesson, students will be equipped with the thinking needed to successfully engage in the inquiry experience.

(Continued)

TABLE 2.1 (Continued)

Teacher:	Yes, I am comfortable with the structure of minilessons. It does mean that I have to think through some of the learning experiences more deeply, especially the texts to be used, so that there is a clear relationship between the content and skill learning targets being taught and the generalization I am unpacking.
Literacy Coach:	Absolutely! This is exactly how we bring more depth to instruction and significantly reduce the time we spend reteaching and reviewing! Down the road, we can look at more specific criteria for evaluating your learning experiences, but for now, you are on track, and I am impressed with your thinking. I am going to leave you with a couple of final questions today: How might you structure the next step in the students' inquiry? How might you differentiate the learning experiences so that you meet the needs of all your students? And how will you assess how well students meet the learning targets of this lesson? See you in a few days.
Session 3	
Literacy Coach:	Michelle, you have been BUSY these past few days! I see you have mapped out the remainder of your learning experiences and more!
Teacher:	Yes, I got into the flow of planning. I have to say, it was with a lot of great dialogue with my colleagues. They were tremendous in helping me locate texts that will work perfectly in this lesson, and with channeling my thinking so I didn't stray away from the "big idea."
Literacy Coach:	That is so important to the process. I know you are going to be a big help to them when they start working on changing their lessons. How about the differentiation question I left you with last session? I see you have identified texts at different levels of readability and interests so that all students have access to the concepts under study. I love the range of topics and media—sports, politics, even cartoon illustrations, and advertisements! Brilliant! You obviously remembered that we can differentiate the process, content, and product of a learning experience but never the target generalization. Bravo!
Teacher:	Yes, I am primarily differentiating the readability of the texts. The real challenge was finding different types with examples that clearly reflect the components of an argument and different types of evidence so all students can be part of the greater conversation and construct the generalization. I'd really like students to interact with various genres so that all learners can access the concepts. An "artifact box" will provide a perfect structure for this. This inquiry will require collaboration, communication, and critical-thinking skills!
Literacy Coach:	I see you have some traditional means of assessing students' skills—like the short quiz on different types of evidence, but what is really impressive is that you didn't let the assessment of understanding drop off. Having students individually create an analogy to expresses the relationship between the *organization of the components of an argument* and the *impact on the author's claim* is a fun and quick way for you to capture each student's conceptual understanding. Deliberately building in your lesson closing is also an indication of how deeply you are thinking about this lesson. I can't wait to pop in and see it all in action!

As a result of my instruction, what is the important conceptual understanding (generalization) I want my students to understand and be able to transfer independently to new situations?

Final Product

Now take a look at how the lesson plan discussion in Table 2.1 came together as a final Concept-Based literacy lesson in Figure 2.6. Remember, when you are first learning about Concept-Based, the process of writing a quality lesson plan will take time but will get easier with practice.

Do you see how the lesson systematically guides students' learning and thinking toward the target generalization *and* addresses knowledge and skills? Facts and skills provide students with the background necessary to construct and later defend the generalization. The third dimension (concepts and a target generalization) enables us to carefully select the facts and skills that will move students' thinking to the generalization. The concepts and generalization give relevance to

(Text continues on page 29.)

FIGURE 2.6 COMPLETED LESSON PLAN

CONCEPT-BASED LESSON PLANNER

Unit Title: *Art of Argumentation*
Grade Level: 10

Instructor: Michelle H.
Lesson Time Frame: approx. 3–5 days

Lesson Opening: (to be communicated with students at lesson onset)

Think of the last time you were in an argument or listened to an argument. Describe what was happening. Was the point of the argument effectively communicated? Was the argument based more on personal opinion and emotions or was support for the claim logically structured, clearly researched (from both sides), and substantiated with factual evidence? Argumentation doesn't need to be viewed as something negative. An argument needn't dissolve into a contest of whose voice is the loudest! Creating an effective argument is an art. In a world that blasts you with information and claims each day, it is important to know what to think, why we think what we do, and how to advance an argument effectively. That's what this unit is about. Are you ready to argue?

Now, think of time or situation that you felt really compelled or convinced by an argument that you heard. Why do you think the argument resonated with you?

Learning Targets: What students will Understand (Generalizations), Know, and be able to Do (Skills)

Generalization(s) (Students will understand that . . .) Note: Generalizations may apply to one or a series of lessons. G#1 indicates the target generalization from the curriculum unit.

Unit G#1 The effective organization of the components of an argument advance an author's claim.

Guiding Questions

1a. What are the components of an argument? (F)
1b. What types of evidence can be used to support the reasons offered in an argument? (specific examples, statistics, data, testimonies, counterclaims, and so on) (F)
1c. What claim is the author (or speaker) of ___ making? (F)
1d. Why is a powerful claim statement important? (C)
1e. How did the author organize the argument presented in the text? (F)
1f. How did the author's organization of the argument impact your understanding of the claim? (F)
1g. How does the organization of the components of an argument impact an author's claim? (C)

Strand	Critical Content (Know)	Key Skills (Able to Do)
Understanding Text	• Central idea vs. specific details • The components of an argument • Types of evidence	CCSS. ELA R19-10.2: Determine a central idea of a text and analyze its development over the course of the text, including how it emerges and is shaped and refined by specific details.
Responding to Text	• Strategies for responding to texts (sticky notes, journal entries, discussion protocols)	CCSS.ELA SL.9-10.3: Evaluate a speaker's point of view, reasoning, and use of evidence and rhetoric, identifying any fallacious reasoning or exaggerated or distorted evidence.
Critiquing Text	• Criteria used to analyze and evaluate an argument • Effective organization of the components of an argument • Valid evidence/reasoning	CCSS. ELA RI.9-10.6 Determine an author's point of view or purpose in a text & analyze how and author uses rhetoric to advance that point of view.
Producing Text	• Traits of effective analogies	CCSS.ELA W.11-12.2.D Use precise language, domain-specific vocabulary, and techniques such as metaphor, simile, and analogy to manage the complexity of the topic.

(Continued)

FIGURE 2.6 (Continued)

Learning Experiences	Differentiation
Capture student responses to Opening question: *Why do you think the argument resonated with you?* on a class T-Chart with headings: *Audience, Claim, Impact.* Add to and revisit this T-Chart through the duration of the unit.	
Minilesson: Create another class anchor chart (to be kept as a visual throughout the unit). Use the chart to introduce the components of an argument, to show relationships to each other, and to guide students to a definition of each component. Guiding Question 1a *What are the components of an argument?* (F) Conduct a Think-Aloud as you read a short argumentative piece. Ask and discuss Guiding Questions 1c. *What claim is the author (or speaker) of ___ making?* (F) and 1d. *Why is a powerful claim statement important?* (C) Reread the short argumentative piece; ask Guiding Question 1e. *How did the author organize the argument presented in the text?* (F) and 1f. *How did the author's organization of the argument impact your understanding of the claim?* (F) Have students use the anchor chart and partner discussion to formulate a response. Share answers to 1f with the whole class.	Think-Aloud provides access to expert thinking
Inquiry: Students continue to investigate the *relationship between* the organization of the components of an argument and advancement of an author's claim. Create small student groups. Distribute an "artifact box" (file) to each group with multiple (5–7) examples of argumentative texts making claims on a variety of topics. Create small student groups. Have student groups study each artifact in the box & then complete a 4 column chart (for each piece of text) with the headings: *Claim, Reasons, Evidence, Counterclaim.* Add these additional concept headings to the class anchor chart and periodically have students add more data from their small-group work. Refer students back to the class anchor chart as it evolves to help them more deeply process information. Pose Guiding Question 1b. *What types of evidence can be used to support the reasons offered in an argument? (specific examples, statistics, data, testimonies, counterclaims, and so forth)* (F) to help students notice patterns in the types of evidence used in the argumentative texts in their artifact boxes. Add types of evidence to the class anchor chart. Have student groups review the 4 column chart through a new lens "Effectiveness of Argument." Pose Guiding Questions 1e. *How did the author organize the argument presented in the text?* (F) and 1f. *How did the author's organization of the argument impact your understanding of the claim?* (F) to analyze the overall impact of the arguments. Students identify the most effective text and share reasons why with small group and class.	Small-group configurations Text examples at different readability levels and different types—Artifact Box: Include 5–7 excerpts from different text sources that exemplify the essential components of effective arguments (for example, articles, cartoons, ads). As needed, provide support/ extension.
Assess: Have students synthesize information from their small group and class chart and individually create an analogy to expresses the relationship between the *organization of the components of an argument* and an author's claim. (G#1)	As needed, provide examples of effective analogies. Sentence stems to scaffold analogy, if needed
Lesson Closing: Reflect on the work completed. Link to where lessons need to go next in the unit.	

Materials/Resources

- Argumentative text to use during Think-Aloud
- 5-7 excerpts from different text sources that exemplify the essential components of effective arguments (for example, articles, cartoons, ads).

Assessments

- Observe the discussion protocols of each group (active participation, on task, questioning, role assignments, and so forth). The observations noted in the students group behaviors will become part of next lesson. (G#5)
- Notice the quality of the students' responses to guiding questions.
- Nongraded pop quiz: Have students list types of evidence as an entry task to connect to the previous learning
- Assess understanding expressed in each analogy.

(Continued from page 26.)

the facts and skills taught in the lesson. We are breaking away from the traditional "coverage" model of using a bank of activities to teach facts and skills that are disconnected from a targeted conceptual understanding. In this teacher's subsequent lessons, instruction will continue to build and extend students' learning. This will be accomplished by designing learning experiences with increasing complexity, which will require students to apply and synthesize facts and skills, look for patterns across examples, analyze concepts, and ultimately construct additional generalizations from the curriculum unit.

Concept-Based Instruction values student intellect.

The impact on student learning reflects the power of Concept-Based Instruction. We guide students to the target generalization, but we also celebrate when students offer and support accurate generalizations in ways we may not have thought of in preplanning. We are teaching students to deeply *understand* what it takes to be a competent, confident, and critical reader, writer, speaker, viewer, researcher, and presenter. Concept-Based Instruction creates a significant departure from students feeling they need to just "get through" each school assignment. Students are held accountable and are far more engaged when the learning experiences require them to investigate concepts, facts, and skills in content that is generative, interesting, and thought-provoking. Concept-Based Instruction values students' intellect. It is designed so that conceptual structures of the brain are being gradually and steadily developed, which makes learning motivating and memorable! Students from Concept-Based classrooms tell us so all the time.

Summary

In Chapter 3, we'll go a step further by explaining how Concept-Based supports an inquiry approach to learning. It is also chock-full of completed literacy lesson plans that dive further into analyzing how they differ from most traditional lessons, and it offers a rubric for assessing how your Concept-Based lesson plans are progressing. You are ready to take another step forward!

Extending Thought

1. What are some of the qualities of a Concept-Based teacher?
2. How and why is lesson design important to supporting inquiry and learning transfer?
3. What are some of the key differences between traditional two-dimensional curriculum and three-dimensional, Concept-Based Curriculum?
4. Earlier Concept-Based books explain the criteria for writing quality generalizations. One criterion requires we not use "No! No!" verbs in a generalization. "No! No!" verbs include: *affect, impact, influence, is, are,* and *have.* Using the graphic in Figure 2.7, explain why these "No! No!" verbs are no-nos.

FIGURE 2.7 STRONG VERB VISUAL

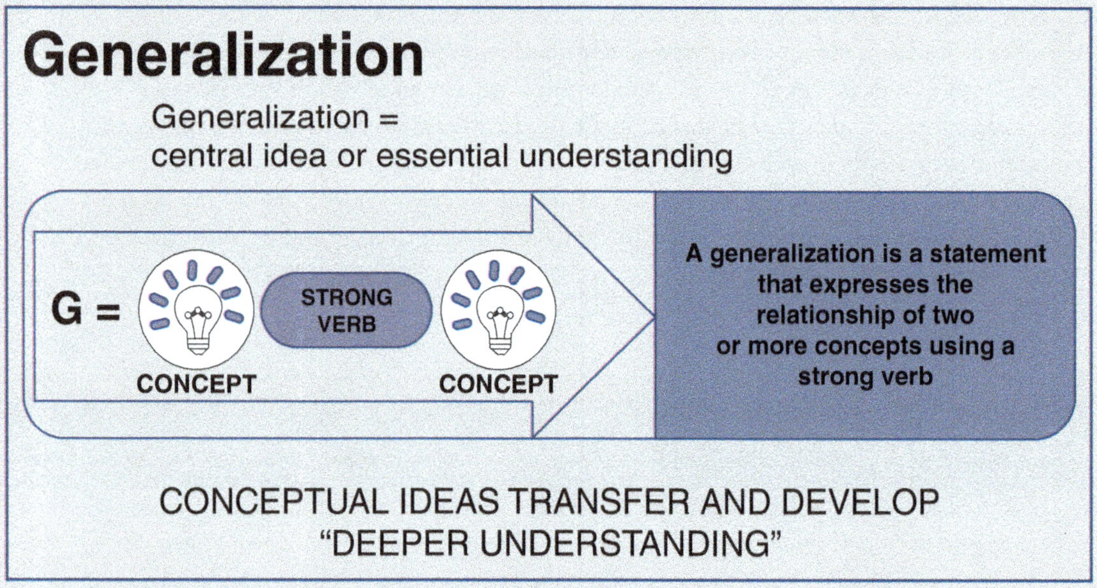

CHAPTER 3

Learning From Model Literacy Lesson Plans

FIGURE 3.1

From the critical components of Concept-Based lesson planning, we now take you on a deep dive into a literacy lesson on multiple fronts. This chapter is richly informative and will make your Concept-Based literacy classroom come alive! There is a lot in here; it includes the following:

- A discussion of the role of inquiry in a literacy classroom, followed by an explanation of how inductive inquiry and explicit skill instruction work together in Concept-Based teaching.
- A blank Concept-Based lesson planner template embedded with Concept-Based lesson-planning rubric criteria to help explain the purpose of each section of the planner.

- Four Model Lessons, centered on different generalizations, each representing a strand of comprehensive, well-balanced literacy instruction. An explanation of the strands comes prior to the lesson examples.
- A Spotlight, in each Model Lesson, of a "tried and true," high-impact literacy practice.
- Questions for you to consider (sprinkled throughout each Model Lesson) to help extend your thinking and deepen your learning about designing Concept-Based lesson plans.
- A brief reflection to wrap up each Model Lesson followed by a progression of generalizations. The progressions are our attempt to emphasize that student learning is a journey, much like our own as Concept-Based teachers. The "whole" or bigger picture must be kept in mind as we invest in our students each day.

Don't let the list above overwhelm you. Each point is interconnected and may include many elements of your current teaching. Sharpening, clarifying, and aligning your understanding are our goals.

Role of Inductive Inquiry in a Concept-Based Literacy Classroom

Literacy teachers traditionally gravitate toward explicit skill development and linear skill progressions. Complex processes are broken into little bits, assuming that this separation will lead to easier mastery. As a result, from the student perspective, learning often feels like a series of isolated skills in disjointed tasks that never come together to form a connected understanding. This cycle may continue year after year until the student has lost all perspective on what it *feels* like to be a proficient reader and writer. How do we avoid this?

One pillar of Concept-Based lesson planning is designing learning experiences that reflect the process of inductive inquiry. The power of inductive inquiry in a literacy classroom shouldn't be underestimated. Inquiry learning experiences in a literacy classroom allows students to be actively engaged in the construction of meaning through the exploration of rich text examples across a range of genres.

In an inductive, inquiry-based learning experience, students:

1. Investigate multiple examples for a specific purpose with a conceptual focus
2. Draw out or identify concepts from the examples
3. Collect evidence and notice patterns across examples (which will serve as support for the generalization)
4. Build a transferable understanding that transfers either within the discipline or beyond the discipline
5. State the understanding in their own words by completing the phrase, "As a result of this investigation, we/I understand that . . .

To move beyond the routine execution of the skills, strategies, and processes, students need opportunities to construct understanding on their own in meaningful and authentic contexts. As we design lesson plans, this goal remains at the forefront of our thinking. If teaching literacy through inquiry is new for you, don't worry; the model lesson plans will provide you with many ideas!

FIGURE 3.2 EXAMPLE OF INDUCTIVE INQUIRY IN A LITERACY CLASSROOM

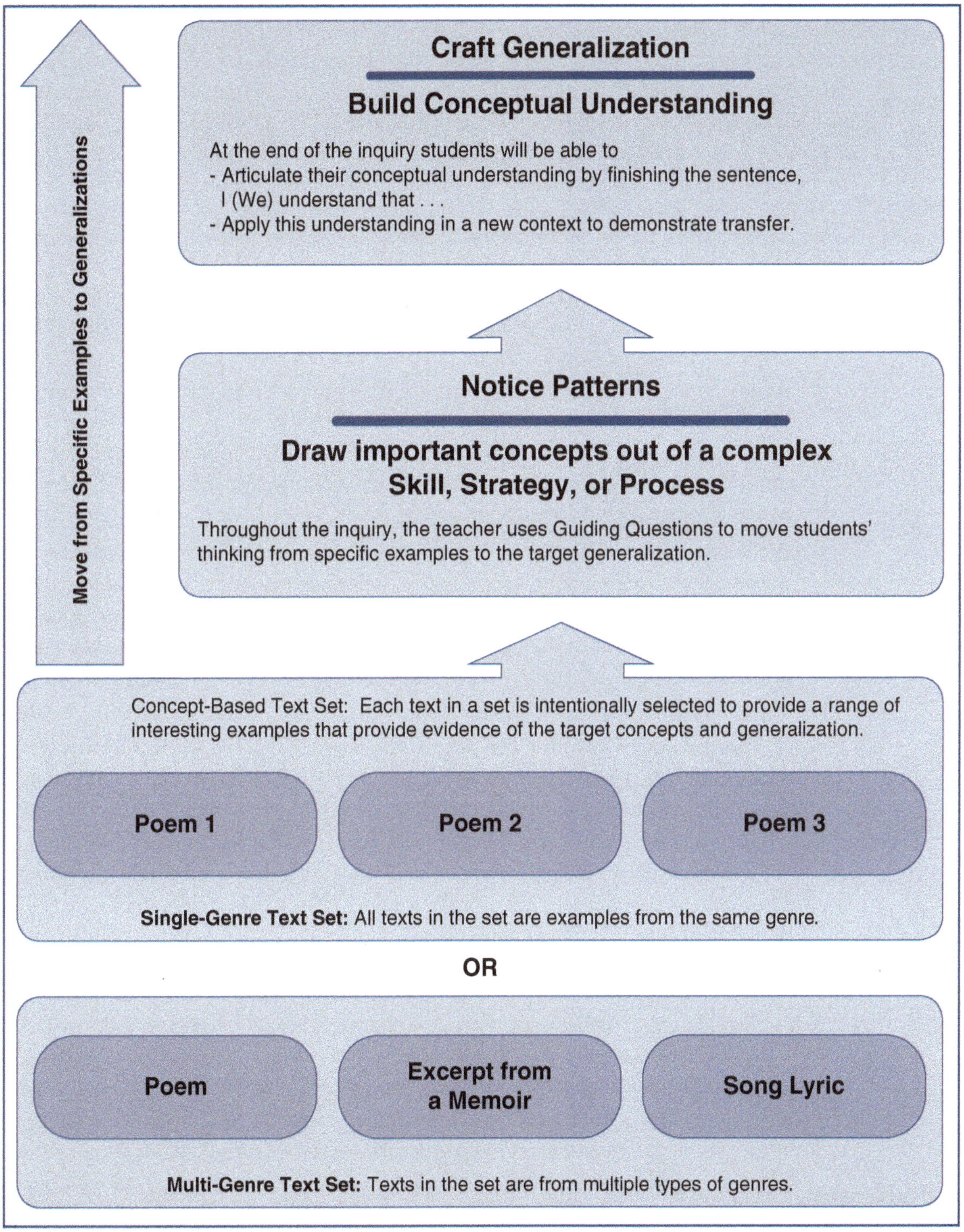

Balancing Inductive Inquiry and Explicit Instruction

Knowing that learning through inquiry is the basis of a Concept-Based literacy classroom, teachers often wonder about the role of explicit skill instruction. CBCI is aligned with the best practices associated with balanced literacy, which include opportunities for explicit instruction before, within, or alongside the inquiry process. In other words, even in a single lesson plan, instruction may incorporate inquiry AND explicit instruction in the context of high-impact literacy practices.

Guided and structured inquiry lessons, as described in Marschall and French's book *Concept-Based Inquiry in Action* (2018), keep the learning of processes, strategies, and skills contextualized; but there are times when processes, strategies, and skills require separate, sequenced, and direct (explicit) instruction. To provide explicit instruction, teachers may temporarily **Pause** the inquiry process, and **Zoom-in** on the specific skill, strategy, or process.

There are many reasons why a teacher might **Pause**, but below are three prevailing practices.

- **A Planned Pause for Daily Small-Group Instruction:** Sometimes explicit instruction occurs in small groups that meet regularly for short strategy lessons. These students **Pause** and step out of the inquiry work briefly for instruction that deliberately targets, or **Zooms-in** on, their skill development. The teacher rotates instruction with 1–2 small groups, daily, in a corner of the room for approximately 20 minutes for a tightly focused skill lesson (Lanning, 2013). Students then jump back into the larger classroom literacy community to actively participate in an inquiry tied to the Concept-Based Curriculum.
- **A Planned Pause Within an Inquiry Lesson (Whole Class):** Teachers can also purposely plan parts of an inquiry lesson where instruction will **Pause & Zoom-in** for the whole class**,** because there are key skills and knowledge (learning targets) that are foundational to the inquiry and require explicit instruction. The key here is knowing when, during the inquiry process, the focus of instruction requires a shift to a specific skill without letting students lose the flow of the inquiry process.
- **A Spontaneous Pause for the Whole Class or a Targeted Group of Students:** In another case, a **Pause** within an inquiry process can be spontaneous, because an unanticipated learning need surfaced. In other words, while students are in the midst of solving a problem or responding to an inquiry question, the teacher notices several students struggling with a particular skill or lacking the appropriate background knowledge important to the inquiry. He quickly **Zooms** his teaching in and explicitly addresses the identified learning need.

In each description above, a **Pause** is just that, a temporary pause. The word *pause* implies that there is something greater going on in the classroom that is paused in order to **Zoom-in** and address a specific skill or knowledge that is lacking. A two-dimensional classroom is not likely to have that "something greater" going on. Rather, in two-dimensional literacy classrooms, explicit instruction may be the only approach. In this case, the goal becomes mastery of specific skills, while conceptual understanding and transfer are assumed rather than deliberately developed and expected. In Concept-Based instruction, students engage in meaningful, motivating inquiry processes with learning experiences that require thinking and develop understanding of how literacy "works." Explicit instruction is alive and well and purposeful, but student learning goes beyond facts and skills.

The word *pause* implies that there is something greater going on in the classroom that is paused in order to Zoom-in and address a specific skill or knowledge that is lacking.

What does **Pause & Zoom-in** look like in practice? The Model Lesson Plans in this chapter show different classroom scenarios where instruction **Zooms-in** on a specific skill.

In each situation, students are developing skills that are meaningful and relevant to their literacy learning. However, conceptual understanding is never out of sight for long. The teacher simply

FIGURE 3.3 BALANCING INDUCTIVE INQUIRY WITH INTENTIONAL SKILL DEVELOPMENT

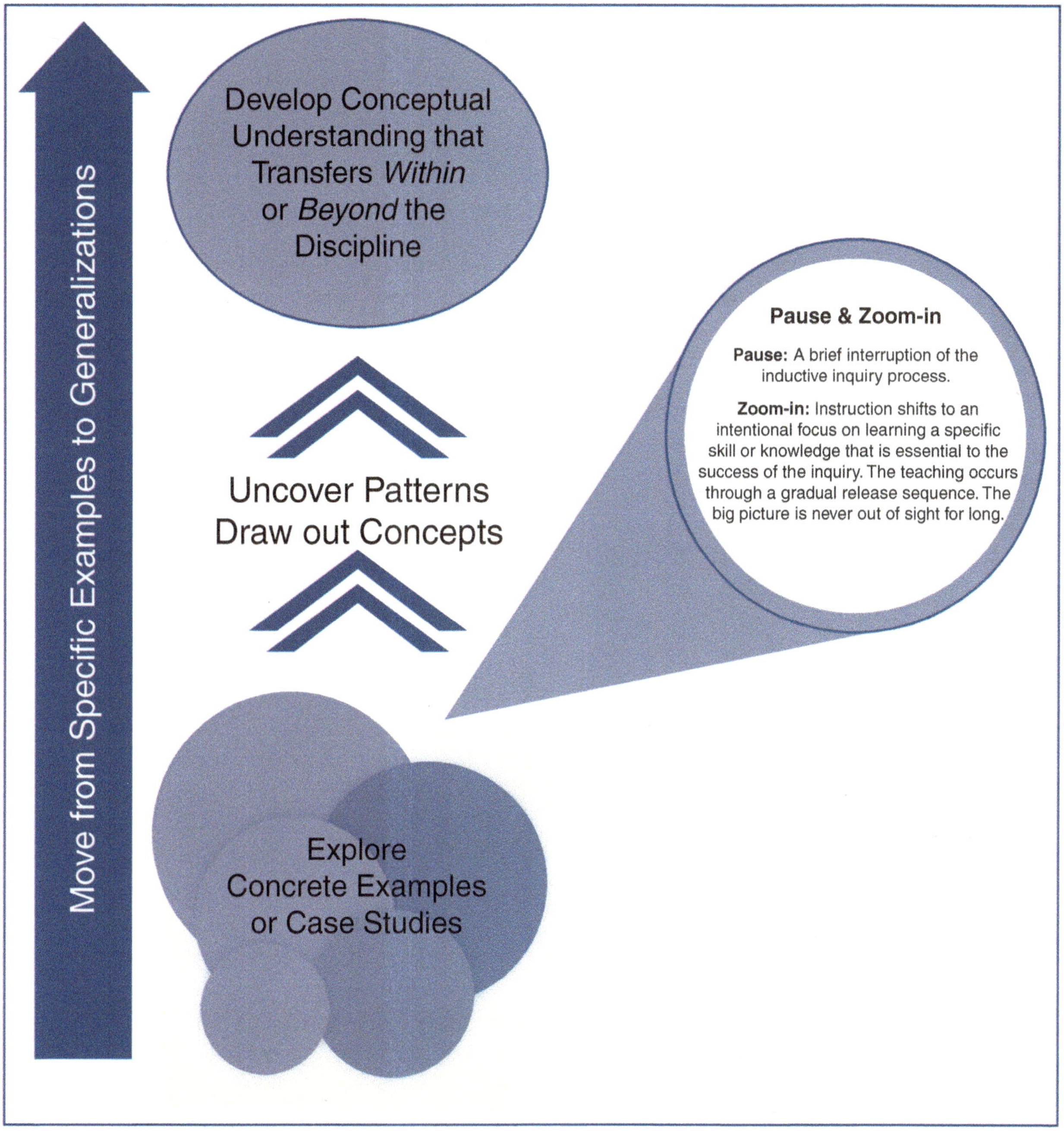

Pauses & Zooms-in, then allows students to continue with their larger inquiry as shown in Figure 3.3. A gradual release framework structures how explicit instruction is delivered. The teacher maintains control at the beginning of the lesson but progressively releases responsibility for the thinking and work to the students, stepping back in with specific, corrective feedback as needed.

The Developing Concept-Based Teacher Rubric

"The Developing Concept-Based Teacher: *Lesson Planning*" rubric (Resource E) is a valuable tool in identifying the critical areas and criteria for designing lessons with fidelity to the tenets of Concept-Based Curriculum and Instruction. This rubric follows the steps of lesson design outlined in Chapter 2 and helps teachers see how they are progressing in their journey to becoming a Master Concept-Based teacher. It may be used in a variety of ways, but, in keeping with the purpose of this chapter, we are correlating each component, first, with a blank lesson planner template, and, later, with model lesson plans to help you better understand how to construct quality Concept-Based instruction.

Correlation Between Concept-Based Lesson Planner Template and the Concept-Based, Lesson-Planning Rubric

Most of the language from the rubric (in the side boxes in Figure 3.4) comes from the "master" Concept-Based lesson planning column, which is the ultimate target. The criteria highlight the

Examples of Pause and Zoom-in

A Spontaneous Pause for the Whole Class or a Targeted Group of Students:

Let's imagine a classroom of ninth graders are conducting an inquiry about author bias in their nonfiction curriculum unit. Since the students are from a rural farming community, many families access water from private wells on properties, so the teacher suggests that students investigate articles about the impact of pesticides used on the locally grown crops. The teacher soon notices that although the students are beginning to flush out text bias, many of the sources students are accessing are out of date. The teacher might say, *"Let's* ***Pause*** *here, and* ***Zoom-in*** *on evaluating sources. Why should we care about the date a website was published?"* After providing explicit instruction on the skill of evaluating sources, the teacher Zooms back out and students continue their inquiry. All students in a class may benefit from a **Pause & Zoom** (as in this scenario), or the teacher may briefly pull together a small group of identified students.

A Planned Pause for Daily, Small Group Instruction:

Here's another example of explicit instruction. A new Concept-Based literature unit was recently launched in this fourth grade classroom. The teacher opens today's literacy block with a minilesson, centering on a learning experience from the curriculum unit that sets up an inquiry task. After 5–7 minutes, the teacher points out the additional literacy assignments to be completed once students have finished their inquiry work for the day, and the students are released from the minilesson to begin their work.

Next, the teacher begins her small-group reading instruction. She meets daily with two groups, on a rotation basis, for approximately 20 minutes each, to explicitly teach ongoing skills. The explicit small-group instruction in and of itself is not the end goal, but rather, it continues to build and strengthen the skills students need to participate in the richer and conceptual inquiry task.

A Planned Pause Within an Inquiry Lesson (Whole Class):

Now, imagine a group of sixth graders exploring the relationship between *personal experience* and *identity*. In this unit, students read several short memoirs of various authors' personal experiences. They are now beginning to craft vignettes that represent significant moments from their childhood and helped to shape their identity. The teacher knows students need explicit instruction in how to conclude their narrative vignettes, as this genre is new to them. Midway through the students' first draft of their personal narratives, the teacher **Pauses and Zooms-in** on techniques for writing personal narrative conclusions. To do this he selects and reads aloud a closing paragraph from one of the memoirs the students previously read. He models his thinking for students: *What do I notice about how this author brought closure to her personal narrative? One thing I see is that the author is reflecting on her experience. What does she want me to take away from her story? I think it is . . . , and so on."* Students are guided through a second example before they are released back to their process writing. Through this **Pause & Zoom**, students discover writing techniques that they can immediately use in their own writing. Now they are prepared to finish writing their personal narratives.

FIGURE 3.4 CONCEPT-BASED LESSON PLANNING TEMPLATE WITH RUBRIC CRITERIA

CONCEPT-BASED LESSON PLANNER

Unit Title: **Instructor:**

Subject: **Grade Level:**

Lesson Number: 1 **Lesson Time Frame:** ______ **days**

Engages synergistic thinking—asks students to consider knowledge/skills through conceptual lens

Lesson Opening: (to be communicated with students at lesson onset):

Learning Targets: What students will Understand (Generalizations), Know and be able to do (Skills)

Generalization(s) (Students will understand that . . .)

Guiding Questions

1a.

1b.

1c.

1d.

1e.

Strand	Critical Content (Know)	Key Skills (Able to Do)
Understanding:		
Responding:		
Critiquing:		
Producing:		

Learning Design:

Lesson design is primarily inductive, requiring students to engage in a multifaceted inquiry process and to reflect on the connections across the examples presented so that students can formulate and defend their generalizations.

A deductive design may also be included to support learning the foundational facts and skills *(Pause & Zoom-in).*

Lesson Opening:

Engages synergistic thinking—asks students to consider knowledge/skills through conceptual question(s) or lens.

Learning Targets

Represent what students are expected to Know, Understand, and Do

NOTE: There will only be 1–2 generalizations per lesson. The focus of inquiry is lost if there are too many generalizations to uncover. There are, however, Critical Content and Key Skill lesson learning targets for each of the 4 unit Strands because students need experiences across all strand modes in order to fully understand the target generalization.

Guiding Questions

Questions are different types (factual, conceptual, debatable) and are listed throughout the plan.

The lesson plan shows a deliberate effort to use questions to help students bridge from the factual to the conceptual level of understanding.

(Continued)

FIGURE 3.4 (Continued)

Learning Experiences

Student work requires students to cognitively wrestle with and synthesize knowledge, skills, and concepts under study in relevant contexts that lead to the realization of the generalization.

Student work is at the appropriate level of challenge, is intellectually and emotionally engaging, meaningful, and relevant to the discipline, and provides appropriate student choice.

Tasks are deliberately designed to enhance the transfer of learning across other disciplines and situations.

Learning Experiences	Differentiation

Differentiation

Plans for differentiation to meet the needs of all learners are included and support all students' meeting a common conceptual understanding (generalization).

Differentiation is based on the analysis of multiple data points that reveal individual student learning needs.

Specific accommodations are readily available based on anticipated student misconceptions and needs.

Materials/Resources:

Assessments:

Closing:

Assessment

Assessment types are varied so they assess students' developing knowledge, skills, and understandings (generalizations) and allow for timely feedback.

Assessments provide relevant information about students' process of learning as well as their learning products.

Student self-assessment is valued.

Closing:

Plans for a way that evidence of learning can be reviewed collectively.

TABLE 3.1 MODEL LESSON GENERALIZATIONS BY STRAND

	Strand	Generalization
Model Lesson Plan 1	Understanding Text	*Collaborative deep text analysis supports the recognition and grasp of allusions by providing new insight and extending understanding.*
Model Lesson Plan 2	Responding to Text	*Discourse enables participants to revise and deepen their current understanding of a topic, idea, or concept.*
Model Lesson Plan 3	Critiquing Text	*An author's purpose, audience, and message direct the best choice of communication medium.*
Model Lesson Plan 4	Producing Text	*Writers create precise images, people, places, and events in a reader's mind through specific words and details.*

intent of each step of lesson planning. As you read, consider how these descriptors are similar to or different from how you typically approach: 1) a lesson's learning targets, 2) your lesson opening, 3) student learning experiences, 4) differentiation, 5) assessments, and 6) lesson closing.

When compared side by side with the lesson plan template, you can see how the rubric criteria from "The Developing Concept-Based Teacher: *Lesson Planning*," serve as benchmarks when writing a lesson. As you work, it may be helpful to translate the descriptors into questions. For example, the lesson opening criterion: "Engages synergistic thinking—asks students to consider knowledge/skills through a conceptual lens," becomes: "Does my lesson opening engage synergistic thinking by asking students to consider knowledge/skills through a conceptual lens?" Your answer to this question then determines your next steps. If you answer yes, continue with your lesson planning. If you answer no, then rethink the lesson opening. What *could* you do to "engage synergistic thinking?" Model Lesson Plan 1 (Fig. 3.5) demonstrates this process.

Learning Through Model Lesson Plans

The four lesson plans in this chapter are not meant to be make-it-take-it lessons, but rather models for you to analyze, imitate, and use as inspiration as you design your lessons for your unique students. In the Resources section of this book, you will find the Concept-Based Curriculum units from which each Model Lesson was crafted. The models also represent lessons at various stages of the curriculum unit implementation.

Each of the Model Lessons centers on a specific generalization, drawn from a curriculum unit. The target generalization in each Model Lesson primarily represents one of the four strands in order to provide examples of all types of literacy lessons. (See Table 3.1)

A lesson spans more than one class (day), because guiding students' thinking to the realization of the target generalization takes time. We don't want to muddy the waters by having too many generalizations in a lesson where the focus of inquiry is lost or becomes confusing. That said, as you read through each lesson, you will notice that even when the emphasis of a lesson generalization is on a particular strand, the natural reciprocity among the four means that learning in other strands is being advanced concurrently through the learning experience.

Model Lesson Plan 1 (drawn from Resource A-3): Understanding Text

Introduction

In a vibrant classroom filled with laughter and energetic eighth graders, students are excited to share with each other all that they are discovering in their novels. Lessons are from their curriculum unit titled "Dystopian Societies: Could this really be our future?" In previous weeks, the students explored the relationship between the setting and the believability of speculative fiction stories and how readers discover the negative elements of dystopian novels through their connections with the protagonist. This week, students are getting ready for their next mini-inquiry in this curriculum unit. The teacher uses a series of guiding questions to help bridge students' thinking about the process of reading from the skill level to the conceptual level. Since the instruction in this classroom represents the three-dimensional Concept-Based model, all students are reading a title selected from a classroom set of multiple dystopian novels. Each student is reading a different novel. The students' individual novels serve as "case studies" as they conduct mini-inquiries designed to help uncover a transferable, conceptual understanding (generalization) that supports their development as capable, discerning readers.

> ***SPOTLIGHT:***
> ***High-Impact Literacy Practice #1***
>
> ***Close Reading***
> **"The practice of close reading, an instructional technique for inspecting a brief passage of text to determine its inferential meaning, is not a new one . . .**
>
> **"The teacher pauses frequently to ask text-dependent questions that cause readers to look back into the text (and thus reread). These are focusing rather than funneling questions, and move from literal to structural and inferential levels of analysis" (Fisher, Frey, & Hattie, 2016, pp. 89–90).**

Students will continue reading and working with their new dystopian novels for the next several weeks—hence, this lesson plan spans about a week of class periods. Taking the time to design a lesson that frames multiple blocks of instruction helps teachers design with the "whole" in mind. The lesson will be "tweaked" daily, based on how students are progressing, but a broader lesson plan breaks away from the "what should I do tomorrow?" mindset. Front-loading planning time results in teaching efficiency and provides time for students to grapple and ponder and discuss as their thinking is guided toward the construction of the lesson generalization. If students can articulate a generalization after a single class period, it most likely means the generalization was not very robust!

Things to Notice as You Read Model Lesson Plan 1:

- How the teacher structures learning through inductive inquiry.
- How the teacher uses the technique of Pause & Zoom-in with guided instruction and minilessons to intentionally develop both skill and conceptual understanding.
- How the teacher uses a single-genre text set, which allows student choice of text and enables "case studies" for students to learn and compare the intricacies of the genre.
- How the teacher encourages students to draw out concepts and notice patterns through periodic Close Reading.
- How the lesson focuses on students' understanding of the reading process, not just the specific text.

Reflection on Model Lesson Plan 1

The first Model Lesson focuses on the Strand *Understanding Text* to address the instruction students continue to need to keep them engaged and thriving as literacy learners. In this well-structured lesson plan, the teacher effectively blends inquiry, explicit instruction, and independent practice, while still allowing students the opportunity to explore and cognitively wrestle with the material. Through Close Reading, students actively notice elements from their own novels, compare with partners, compare in table groups, and generalize as a class. The use of a simple graphic organizer like Resource B-1 can help students organize information and notice patterns. In the final step, students are given the chance to put the understanding gained through this learning experience into their own words by crafting a generalization. Students began by identifying key concepts and used two or more of the concepts in a statement of relationship with the sentence starter, "We understand that . . . " as a tool to express their thinking in terms of conceptual understanding.

The conceptual understanding, gained through mini-inquiries such as this, is transferable; thus, it can apply to any book the student is reading now, and in the future. If all students are reading the same book, they no longer have the opportunity to look for a range of different patterns. One text for all locks learning to a specific text and to a specific author. Students are denied the opportunity to generalize, explore diverse texts, and develop their own conceptual understanding. By using the generalization as a specific target for instruction, by incorporating peer collaboration, and by providing a choice in texts, students use the skills, strategies, and texts to come to a deeper understanding of the reading and writing process.

FIGURE 3.5 MODEL LESSON PLAN 1

CONCEPT-BASED MODEL LESSON 1

Unit Title: *Dystopian Societies: Could this really be our future?*
Grade Level: 8
Lesson Number: 2 **Lesson Time Frame:** 7–9 days

Lesson Opening: (to be communicated with students at lesson onset)

Through our exploration of our dystopian novels, we are beginning to realize that the perfect societies created in our stories are not so perfect after all . . . a darker side is becoming apparent! We began the unit by exploring how the content of dystopian novels creates a world that seems believable to the reader. We came to understand that *"The believability of science-speculative fiction stories increases when the new world contains a blend of realistic and unrealistic elements."* [Teacher points to the generalization posted on chart paper] Last week, we explored the role that the protagonist plays in helping the reader discover the negative elements of the society. You came up with the generalization: *Readers discover the negative elements of a dystopian society through connections with the struggles of a protagonist.*
[Again, teacher points to where the generalizations are posted on chart paper on the wall.]

How does this lesson opening engage students' minds and interests?

Now, we are going to start digging even deeper and really hone in, as readers, on our text analysis skills. This will not only increase your ability to more deeply understand literature, but it will also help you become more critical consumers of the things you encounter in the world around you. You will become master detectives as you make discoveries of those hidden messages that readers often overlook. Nothing will get by you! You will be amazed at all you can learn from your novel through the process we call Close Reading. Close Reading requires you, as a reader, to deeply analyze text. Let's get started.r

How does this lesson opening connect to and extend previous thinking?

Learning Targets: What students will Understand (Generalizations), Know and be able to Do (Skills)

Generalization(s) (Students will understand that . . .) Note: Generalizations may apply to one or a series of lessons. #G indicates the target generalization from the curriculum unit.

Unit G#4 *Collaborative deep text analysis supports the recognition and grasp of allusions by providing new insights and extending understanding.*

How does using a generalization as a learning target help ensure instruction is designed to support conceptual understanding?

Guiding Questions

4a. What is deep analysis of a text? (F)
4b. What strategies are important when collaborating with others in deep text analysis? (F)
4c. What is an allusion? (F)
4d. How does an author's use of allusions change reading expectations? (C)
4e. How can collaborative deep text analysis help uncover meaning that may have been previously unnoticed? (C)
4f. How can collaborative deep text analysis provide new insights and extend understanding? (C)
4g. Why do some texts lend themselves to collaborative deep analysis more than others? (C)
4h. What are the potential consequences of not deeply analyzing complex text? (D)

How do the guiding questions help students reach a conceptual level of understanding?

Strand	Critical Content (Know)	Key Skills (Able to Do)
Understanding Text	• Definition of allusion • Strategies for deep text analysis	CCSS.ELA-LITERACY.RL.8.1: Cite the textual evidence that most strongly supports an analysis of what the text says explicitly as well as inferences drawn from the text. CCSS.ELA-LITERACY.RL.8.9: Analyze how a modern work of fiction draws on themes, patterns of events, or character types from myths, traditional stories, or religious works such as the Bible, including describing how the material is rendered new.
Responding to Text	• Collaborative discussion protocols • Perspectives—interpretation	CCSS.ELA-LITERACY.SL.8.1: Engage effectively in a range of collaborative discussions (one-on-one, in groups, and teacher-led) with diverse partners on grade 8 topics, texts, and issues, building on others' ideas and expressing their own clearly.
Critiquing Text	• Author's intent • Connotation	CCSS.ELA-LITERACY.RL.8.4: Determine the meaning of words and phrases as they are used in a text, including figurative and connotative meanings; analyze the impact of specific word choices on meaning and tone, including analogies or allusions to other texts.
Producing Text	• Text evidence • Elaboration	CCSS.ELA-LITERACY.L.8.3: Use knowledge of language and its conventions when writing, speaking, reading, or listening.

(*Continued*)

FIGURE 3.5 (Continued)

Learning Experiences	Differentiation
Review and Pre-Assessment: Ask students to reflect on the reading strategies they use for comprehending complex texts versus how they read less challenging texts. Ask students what they think about the meaning of the terms: <u>Deep Text Analysis</u> and <u>Surface Reading</u>: Create a T-chart comparing the characteristics of each term. First brainstorm individually, then compare ideas with table groups. Collect group responses on a chart for the wall.	**As you read the description of differentiation that follows, think about this: How does this lesson support the needs of all learners in meeting a common conceptual understanding?**
<u>Mini-Inquiry:</u> Let students know that in their new dystopian novel they will go beyond the literal interpretation of the text to discover the hidden references and deeper meanings that the author uses to communicate his/her message. The focus will be on the concepts of *Deep Text Analysis* and *Allusion*. Distribute excerpts from different types of texts (containing allusions) to each group. Have students first read excerpt independently. After initial read, ask students to: • Identify what the texts have in common (each text references something beyond the text) • Pose and guide general responses to: *What is an allusion?* (GQ#4c) • Reread the groups' excerpt and circle any allusions (references beyond the text) • Each table discusses why the author may have used this allusion.	**Methods of differentiation throughout the lesson:** Graphic organizers and sentence starters as determined by individual needs. Opportunities for students to process thinking verbally.
Guided Instruction: **[Teacher scaffolds questions as needed, periodically gives students time to share their thinking with a partner before reporting out.]** Read aloud ______ text excerpt. • *What is an example of an allusion or hidden reference in this text?* • *How do we know that is an allusion?* Reread an allusion from text. • *What can we infer about this allusion?* • *What do we know about _______?* • *Why would the author use it?* • *What meaning or insight did his or her allusion add for you as the reader?* • *What strategies did you use to unpack the allusion? How did hearing the thinking of others help you understand the allusion?* • *How does an author's use of allusions change reading expectations?* (GQ#4d) [The writer expects the reader to have enough knowledge to recognize the allusion and infer its importance in a text.] • *What strategies are important when collaborating with others in deep text analysis?* (GQ#4b) • *Can more be added now to your understanding of the difference between Deep Text Analysis and Surface Reading?* **Summary:** Readers use Deep Text Analysis to uncover hidden references in complex text. A few words can have a major impact on how a reader interprets and understands the author's message.	Text set contains examples that all students can access, including visual and artistic expressions. Students self-select dystopian novels. Range of text options including varied reading levels, and topics based on student interests. Provide audio versions of the text. Two options for processing charts. One provides additional scaffolding and sentence starters.
Mini-Inquiry and Independent Practice: Ask students to notice how, at different points in their dystopian novel, they will engage in deep analysis of their reading, and, other times, surface level reading. Reminder: *The challenge for readers is to become fluent in the ability to flow back and forth between deep text analysis and reading for pleasure.* Pose the question: *What are the potential consequences of not deeply analyzing complex text?* (GQ#4h) [students will revisit their initial responses later.] Have students engage in daily reading, and each day record evidence of Allusions using a Processing Chart, such as Resource B-1. <u>Column 1</u>: Text Detail and page # (for example, "Oh, so you think you are Einstein?"); <u>Column 2</u>: Writer's Craft–What was the author referring to? (for example, A Famous Person); <u>Column 3</u>: Reader's Craft–How did you as a reader uncover and make sense of this detail or hidden meaning? (for example, Background knowledge, context clues) At the opening of each day, model how you are completing your Processing Chart. [Teacher uses the dystopian novel he/she is personally reading.] Read a short excerpt of text, model questions and thinking aloud, then record the evidence in chart. During the remainder of the class time, monitor and support students through individual conferences. Give students opportunities at the end of class each day to reflect, compare, discuss, and add to their Processing Charts with their small group.	Check-in with individual students on a daily basis and provides scaffolding through questions as determined by need. Discusses discoveries with individual students before having them share in table groups to help those students prepare for the group discussion.

Assessment: Ask students to individually cut their responses from Column 1 of their Processing Chart into horizontal strips to allow for easier sorting. In table groups, ask students to discuss, sort, and create categories for their collective text details. Have students create a label for each category on a sticky note. • Example: "My story made a reference to the American Civil War. Did anyone else notice references to events from history? Let's create a label: Historical Events." • Example: "My story referenced a scene from Alice in Wonderland. Let's create a label: Other Books." Collect categories across groups and take students back to their initial definition of Allusion: *Looking at all the categories of Allusions you found in your texts, can we add anything to our original definition?* [Student findings: An allusion is a quick reference to a person, place, thing or idea of historical, cultural, literary or political significance beyond the text at hand. The person or thing is not described in detail. It is just a little detail inserted into the text.] Ask students to repeat the sorting process from strips of the remaining two columns from their Processing Charts. Pose the question . . . *How can collaborative deep text analysis help uncover meaning that may have been previously unnoticed?* (GQ#4e) Have students reflect individually, compare thinking with a partner, and share out with whole class. Ask students to hold silent written conversations about the following question: *What are the potential consequences of not deeply analyzing text?(GQ#4g-h)* • Students respond to the question individually on the top of a blank sheet of notebook paper for a 2 minute Quick Write. • Students then engage in a silent written conversation as they rotate their sheets of notebook paper around the table group. Each student reads the responses of the students that came before them, then they add to and extend the thinking. • Once all table group members have responded to each student's initial response and the response that followed, they have permission to speak about their written conversation. • Groups then share with the whole class the highlights of their written conversations. • Students revisit the initial brainstorm from the first day of the lesson sequence and add new understanding about the process of deep text analysis. • Ask: *How can collaborative deep text analysis provide new insights and extend understanding?* (GQ#4f) • Have students individually craft a statement of their conceptual understanding (generalization) and add to poster on wall.	Strategic student grouping **How does the process of sorting help students identify patterns?** **How was this series of learning experiences deliberately designed to enhance the transfer of learning?**

Materials/Resources

- Examples of allusions across a variety of text styles and genres
- Class set of dystopian novels
- Dystopian novel for teacher model lesson
- Poster paper for wall chart
- Student handout/graphic organizers to record discoveries
- Small slips of paper
- Prepared graphic organizers with extra scaffolding based on student need
- Notebook paper for t-charts, and written conversation

Assessment:
See lesson plan

Vertical Progressions Support Coherence

Model Lesson 1 introduced you to analyzing Concept-Based lesson planning. This was a Grade 8 lesson. Across Concept-Based Curriculum units, Generalizations are written as progressions. In Table 3.2, you can see how generalizations from curriculum units in previous and subsequent grade levels will continuously support and extend students' conceptual understanding in this strand. Curriculum coherence is vitally important if we want to deliberately build students' subject area expertise and deepen their understanding and retention of literacy learning.

TABLE 3.2 VERTICAL PROGRESSION FOR MODEL LESSON 1

	Grade 5	Model Lesson Plan- Grade 8	Grade 10
Generalization (Understanding Strand)	*Figurative language requires readers to think and use strategies to appreciate the meaning an author is communicating.*	*Collaborative deep text analysis supports the recognition and grasp of allusions by providing new insight and extending understanding.*	*Reliable evidence, uncovered by close reading, may stimulate reevaluation and revision of an existing understanding.*

Model Lesson Plan 2 (drawn from Resource A-4): Responding to Text

SPOTLIGHT:
High-Impact Literacy Practice #2

Student-Led Dialogic Learning
"Exposure to the knowledge, ideas, and perspectives of others, particularly when these do not align with those of the person being exposed, fosters cognitive growth when given the space and tools for sense making" (Fisher, Frey, Hattie, & Thayre, 2017, p. 99).

Introduction

In a unit titled *Every Voice Counts: The Struggle for Equity*, seventh-grade students are asking themselves, "How do I use my voice to raise awareness of important issues?" They are exploring the relationship between effective communication and clarity as they investigate struggles for equity around the world, including access to education, water, shelter, food, family and love, and economic opportunities. In inquiry groups, students will read and analyze resources to build understanding of the topic, while gaining a deeper understanding of the qualities and characteristics of informational texts that communicate information for the reader with clarity. A heavy emphasis is placed on student-led dialogic learning and developing an understanding of the value of collegial discussion in deepening and revising thinking. In this lesson, students begin to realize the power of communication and collaboration.

Things to Notice as You Read Model Lesson Plan 2:

- How the teacher blends teacher-led dialogic instruction with student-led dialogic learning.
- How students are given appropriate choice and input into the direction of their learning within the framework of the unit.
- Learning is focused on understanding a process (such as responding to text) that promotes the transfer of learning to new situations.

Reflection on Model Lesson Plan 2

The second Model Lesson focuses on the Strand *Responding to Text* to demonstrate the essential role that thinking, reflection, collaboration, and communication play in developing conceptual understanding. When student voices are valued and when students are given appropriate choice in their learning, engagement levels soar. Learning focused on a process promotes student choice because different topics and texts can be adjusted each year. In this lesson students investigate struggles for equity around the world, but the learning is not just about the topic. Rather, the lesson deepens students' understanding about what it means to be an effective communicator and a close reader. To honor student interests, the teacher could easily change topics next year. Not only did students engage in meaningful discourse, but they are also given the opportunity to reflect on the value of such conversations.

FIGURE 3.6 MODEL LESSON PLAN 2

CONCEPT-BASED MODEL LESSON 2

Unit Title: *Every Voice Counts: The struggle for equity*
(inspired from unit designed by Burlington-Edison School District, Burlington, WA, USA)
Grade Level: 7 **Lesson Time Frame:** 3–4 days

Lesson Opening: (to be communicated with students at lesson onset)

What does it mean to *thrive* vs. *survive*? What does it take for people to *thrive* in their lives, not just *survive* in their lives. Take a moment to reflect on this individually, and then you will share your thinking with a partner. Write your initial thinking on a sticky note, and place the sticky note under the *Before* column, on our class chart labeled *Before* and *After*. Throughout this unit, we will continue revising our chart. Once you are finished, think about this: "Why is discourse important?"

Learning Targets: What students will Understand (Generalizations), Know and be able to Do (Skills)

Generalization(s) (Students will understand that . . .) Note: Generalizations may apply to one or a series of lessons. G# indicates the target generalization from the curriculum unit.

Unit G#2) Readers analyze the development of the central idea of a text to create an objective summary.

2a. What is the central idea(s) of your text? Support with evidence. (F)
2b. What reading strategies helped you determine the central idea(s)? (F)
2c. How did the author of your article develop the central idea(s) across the text? (F)
2d. What is "an objective summary" of text? (F)
2e. What skills support crafting an objective summary of a text? (F)
2f. How does analyzing how the central idea(s) of text is developed vs. simply identifying the central ideas(s) help ensure a summary will be objective? (C)
2g. Why are objective summaries of text important? (C)

Unit G#3) Discourse enables participants to revise and deepen their current understanding of a topic, idea, or concept.

3a. What does a respectful conversation look like and sound like? (F)
3b. What did someone say during your group conversation that caused you to think differently about the topic? (F)
3c. What role does discourse play in understanding a text? (C)
3d. Why is it necessary to revise thinking? (C)
3e. Do we always have to accept the ideas of others? (D)

Strand	Critical Content (Know)	Key Skills (Able to Do)
Understanding Text	• Key vocabulary: strive and thrive • Central ideas • Elements of an objective summary	CCSS.ELA-LITERACY.RI.7.2: Determine two or more central ideas in a text and analyze their development over the course of the text; provide an objective summary of the text.
Responding to Text	• Procedures of collegial-Socratic discussions • Relevant and different types of questions • Sentence starters to provoke elaboration	CCSS.ELA-LITERACY.SL.7.1C: Pose questions that elicit elaboration and respond to others' questions and comments with relevant observations and ideas that bring the discussion back on topic as needed.
Critiquing Text	• Value of various presentation media formats and visuals	CCSS.ELA-LITERACY.SL.7.2: Analyze the main ideas and supporting details presented in diverse media and formats (for example, visually, quantitatively, orally) and explain how the ideas clarify a topic, text, or issue under study.
Producing Text	• Paragraph organization: topic sentence, details, elaborations, closing sentence	CCSS.ELA-LITERACY.W.7.2: Write informative/explanatory texts to examine a topic and convey ideas, concepts, and information through the selection, organization, and analysis of relevant content.

Learning Experiences	Differentiation
G#3: Inquiry into the relationship between discourse and a reader's understanding Students brainstorm answers to GQ 3a. *What does a respectful conversation look like and sound like? (F)*	Scaffold close reading as needed by individual students Audio support
Close Reading (see Fisher, Frey, Hattie, & Thayre, 2017) **Text Selection**—Select an article related to the topic of Struggles for Equity Around the World. The text should be challenging, targeted to the interests of the class, and provoke students' thinking. **Initial Reading**—Students focus on the gist, or constructing basic meaning. **Annotation**—Students read and annotate using the method of annotation previously taught in class. **Repeated Reading**—Students reread the article focusing on gaining a deeper meaning and answering questions marked during annotation. **Responding to Texts**—Prepare for Socratic Seminar. Ask students to write three questions to be posed during the discussion. Review sentence stems for posing questions, and respond to the questions of others. Include a variety of language complexity levels to meet each student at an appropriate level.	**Why is Socratic Seminar an effective technique to allow students to cognitively wrestle with and synthesize the knowledge, skills, and concepts under study?**
Hold Socratic Seminar Distribute a reference sheet with the academic conversation sentence stems previously discussed. Students form an inner circle and an outer circle. Swap positions halfway through. Students pose and respond to questions, directing the flow of the conversations independently. Try to refrain from directing the conversation unless necessary. Allow students to wrestle with the text.	Sentence stems to support academic discourse
Reflection after Socratic Seminar Students complete a reflection and self-assessment (Resource C-3) including GQ# 3b, 3c. and 3d: GQ#3b. *What did someone say during your group conversation that caused you to think differently about the topic? (F)* GQ#3c. *What role does discourse have in understanding a text? (C)* GQ#3d. *Why is it necessary to revise thinking? (C)*	**Why is reflective thinking important?**
End of Lesson Discussion Ask GQ#3e. *Do we always have to accept the ideas of others? (D)* Students first discuss with a shoulder partner, then share out as a class.	
G#2: Inquiry Into an Author's Development of the Central Ideas of a Text Create a single genre text set of nonfiction articles about struggles for equity around the world. **Examples of Struggles for Equity:** • Access to education • Access to family and love • Access to clean water • Access to food • Access to shelter • Access to economic opportunities Students form inquiry pairs. Student pairs select one article from a single genre text set. Students read and analyze the text to determine, GQ#2a. *What is the central idea(s) of your text? Support with evidence. (F)* Ask student pairs to now think about, GQ#2b. *What reading strategies helped you determine the central idea(s)? (F)* First ask students to reflect on their reading and discuss with a partner what they did as a reader to help uncover the central idea. Partners now investigate GQ#2c. *How did the author of your article develop the central idea(s) across the text? (F)* Students can use a graphic organizer to help organize their thinking as they respond. Share with class and create a master list or anchor chart for the class. Brainstorm as a class answers to GQ#2d., 2e. *What is "an objective summary" of text? (F) What skills support crafting an objective summary of a text? (F)* Have students write a 1–2 paragraph objective summary of their article.	**How does a single genre text set allow for appropriate levels of challenge, intellectual and emotional engagement, and appropriate student choice?** Use more explicit teaching, questioning and modeling as needed for support and/or extension.

Now that you have read your article, analyzed how the author developed the central idea, and written an objective summary, use the collaborative discussion behaviors you learned earlier and get back in your small inquiry groups to discuss GQ#2f. *How does analyzing how the central idea(s) of text is developed vs. simply identifying the central ideas(s) help ensure a summary will be objective? (C)* Return to opening question: What does it mean to *thrive* vs. *survive*? What does it take for people to *thrive* in their lives, not just *survive* in their lives. Now that you have learned more about the difference, take a moment to reflect on this individually, then share your thinking with a partner. Write your current thinking on a sticky note, and place the sticky note under the *After* column on our class chart. Final class discussion: GQ#2g *Why are objective summaries of text important? (C)* On an exit slip, students write a generalization explaining the relationship between an *analysis, a central idea, and an objective summary.*	**Why is it essential to create learning experiences for students that address Understanding, Responding, Critiquing, and Producing Text in every lesson?**

Materials/Resources
- Articles related to the topic
- Sticky notes
- Sentence stems for academic conversations
- Before, During, and After anchor chart

Assessment:
- Review annotations from close reading
- Observations of conversations during partner, small group, and whole class discussions
- Socratic Seminar Reflection and Self-Assessment
- Exit slip

The technique of Socratic Seminar was strategically selected to help students understand the relationship between discourse and the revision of thinking. Often students reflect on the topic after the Socratic Seminar, but not the process of being a speaker and listener. Concept-Based learners reflect on the process and product to help develop an understanding of *why* we do what we do as readers, writers, speakers, listeners, and viewers.

Vertical Progressions Support Coherence

Model Lesson 2 provides an example of Concept-Based learning in a Grade 7 classroom. As we noted in Model Lesson 1, in Concept-Based Curriculum units, we write generalizations as progressions so that as students move through the K–12 system, teachers are providing learning experiences to deepen conceptual understanding. Ensuring that curriculum is vertically aligned allows students the opportunity to discover the intricacies of a discipline, one well-planned year at a time. In English language arts, concepts such as *discourse* remain constant across the grades, but a student's understanding of the microconcepts in discourse must increase with age and maturity. In the vertical progression below, notice how the concept of discourse is taught each year, yet the intentional use of additional microconcepts ensures that students are deepening their understanding to become more effective communicators.

TABLE 3.3 VERTICAL PROGRESSION FOR MODEL LESSON 2

Model Lesson Plan			
	Grade 4	Grade 7	Grade 9
Generalization (Responding Strand)	*Effective discourse counts on participants sharing ideas and considering the ideas of others.*	*Discourse enables participants to revise and deepen their current understanding of a topic, idea, or concept.*	*Effective discourse challenges participants to respond to diverse perspectives, justify their own views, and make new connections in light of the evidence and reasoning presented.*

Model Lesson Plan 3 (drawn from Resource A-5): Critiquing Text

> *SPOTLIGHT:*
> *High-Impact Literacy Practice #3*
>
> *Extended Writing*
> "Writing is the result of knowledge construction. Evidence of a student's transfer of knowledge can be found in the extended writing pieces he or she creates. Writing instruction, like reading, is a constellation of approaches, as students move from ideas (surface), to thinking (deep), to constructing knowledge (transfer)" (Fisher, Frey, & Hattie, 2016, p. 124).

Introduction

A commitment to the development of students as autonomous, informed thinkers becomes more essential as technologies flood people around the world with daily renderings of events, information, and opinions. The critical evaluation of these ideas, arguments, and points of view is essential to distinguish what is true and what isn't, to know whose voice we can trust, and to uncover sources behind information. The critiquing strand of Concept-Based Curriculum and Instruction lays the foundation for this dimension of literacy learning and continues to "grow it" from the time students enter school until they graduate.

Students in this ninth-grade classroom are spending a few weeks thinking about the choices authors make and the impact those choices have on readers. By this time, students are progressing in their knowledge and understanding of what it takes to be a critical evaluator of information. In this unit, they also learn how they can leverage this understanding to advance their own arguments and points of view. As you read through the full unit (in the Resource section) and the model lesson below, consider how students are being prepared to be thoughtful, informed citizens.

Things to Notice as You Read Model Lesson Plan 3:

- How the teacher uses authentic resources to represent the concepts under study.
- How the teacher creates opportunities for dynamic literacy discussions after students have time to individually process information.
- How the teacher uses Tracking Thinking Charts to help students see how their thinking grows and changes throughout the lesson.
- How the teacher uses Extended Writing to see how students are able to synthesize their learning and to assess their conceptual understanding.

Reflection on Model Lesson Plan 3

The third Model Lesson focuses on the Strand *Critiquing Text* to highlight the importance of how we need to interact with the world as critical consumers of information. Through this collaborative mini-inquiry, the ninth-grade students analyze two different mediums, addressing the same topic, and how medium impacts subject representation. Students are active readers, writers, speakers, listeners, and viewers as they investigate the authentic topics and mediums.

At the conclusion of their work, the teacher assigned Extended Writing and asked students to express a transferable, conceptual understanding about the medium choices authors make and the consequences of those choices on the message and audience. The teacher did not make assumptions about what the students understand and will be able to transfer as a result of their learning experience; rather, the teacher specifically pushed the lesson through to three-dimensional instruction.

Vertical Progressions Support Coherence

Generalizations that may be targeted in grades leading up to this Model Lesson are in Table 3.4. We need to consider students traveling from grade level to grade level to ensure

FIGURE 3.7 MODEL LESSON PLAN 3

CONCEPT-BASED MODEL LESSON 3

Unit Title: Oh The Choices Authors Face!
Grade Level: 9 **Lesson Time Frame**: 5 days

Lesson Opening: (to be communicated with students at lesson onset)

In our current unit, we have been examining many of the choices authors make and the impact of those choices— intended or unintended—on the reader. Today, we are going to look at another choice authors make—the choice about medium.

"The medium is the message." Marshall McLuhan first coined this phrase in the 1960s book titled *Understanding the Media: The Extensions of Man*. He wrote at a time when we didn't have many of the communication technologies we have today, but his message remains highly relevant. Let's start by thinking about these questions: What are some of the different mediums you rely on for information? Does medium affect your interest and understanding of a subject or topic? How do authors decide which type to use?

Over the next several classes, you will be conducting a series of mini-inquiries. You will have new text(s) for each inquiry. Your responsibility is to collaborate and engage in meaningful discourse as you and your teammates analyze a range of subjects, across a variety of mediums, while deepening your understanding of the concepts under study: *medium* and *subject representation.*

Learning Targets: What students will Understand (Generalizations), Know and be able to Do (Skills)

Generalization(s) (Students will understand that . . .) Note: Generalizations may apply to one or a series of lessons. G# indicates the target generalization from the curriculum unit.

Unit G#4: An author's purpose, audience, and message direct the best choice of communication medium.

4a. What are examples of different types of communication mediums? (F)
4b. What details of the subject_______________are represented in the first medium example (e.g., print)? What details remain the same or change when this same subject is represented in a different medium? (e.g., video clip)? (F)
4c. How do different mediums shape how a subject is represented? (C)
4d. How is an author's purpose reflected in his/her choice of medium? (C)
4e. Can one medium be relied on more than another to accurately represent a subject? (D)

How do the guiding questions help students reach a conceptual level of understanding?

Strand	Critical Content (Know)	Key Skills (Able to Do)
Understanding Text	• Effective reading strategies • Author's purpose	CCSS.ELA-LITERACY.RL.9-10.4: Determine the meaning of words and phrases as they are used in a text, including figurative connotative, and technical meanings; analyze the cumulative impact of specific word choices on meaning and tone.
Responding to Text	• Protocols for effective discussions • Group member responsibilities	CCSS.ELA.LITERACY.SL.910.1D: Respond thoughtfully to diverse perspectives, summarize points of agreement and disagreement, and, when warranted, qualify or justify their own views and understanding and make new connections in light of the evidence and reasoning presented. CCSS.ELA-LITERACY.SL.9-10.1.A: Come to discussions prepared, having read and researched material under study; explicitly draw on that preparation by referring to evidence from texts and other research on the topic or issue to stimulate a thoughtful, well-reasoned exchange of ideas.
Critiquing Text	• Effect of different types of medium • Impact of the different choices authors make	CCSS.ELA-LITERACY.RL.9-10.7: Analyze the representation of a subject or a key scene in two different artistic mediums, including what is emphasized or absent in each treatment). CCSS.ELA-LITERACY.RI9-10.7: Analyze various accounts of a subject told in different mediums (for example, a person's life story in both print and multimedia), determining which details are emphasized in each account.
Producing Text	• Language conventions in different mediums	CCSS.ELA-LITERACY.L.8.3: Use knowledge of language and its conventions when writing, speaking, reading, or listening.

(Continued)

FIGURE 3.7 (Continued)

Learning Experiences	Differentiation
Mini-Inquiry 1—Tracking Thinking: Assign students to groups of 3–5. Provide each group with one piece of poster paper. [One piece of poster paper encourages more collaboration and shared thinking.] Ask each group to create a visual depiction of their current understanding of the relationship among the concepts: author's purpose, types of media, and subject representation. Students should do this in black marker.	Ideas for differentiation: • Provide groups with texts at varying levels of complexity • Select a range of mediums to allow for multiple points of access or ways to process the concepts understudy, for example, artwork vs. print-based text • Intentionally plan collaborative teams based on the assets each team member could bring to the group • Provide sentence stems to support academic discourse
Mini-Inquiry 2—Analyzing: • Provide texts on the same subject to small groups of students in two different mediums. Ask: GQ#4a. *What are examples of different types of communication mediums?* Share responses. • Have students initially read, view, or hear both versions individually. Next, ask students to identify and record in a Venn diagram the *significant* differences of the subject's representation in the two versions—GQ#4b. *What details were changed, added, or deleted from the original? What stayed the same?* • Ask each group to use information from their completed Venn diagram to discuss GQ#4c. *How do different mediums shape how a subject is represented?* And, GQ#4d. *How is an author's purpose reflected in his/her choice of medium?* • After time for discussion, hand out a new color of marker and ask each group to update their thinking on the poster paper used in **Mini-Inquiry 1.** • Ask groups to summarize the shifts in their thinking and understanding with the class. • Ask, what do you now understand about the relationship between the concepts of: *medium, author's purpose* and *subject representation* that you didn't before? • After class sharing, groups edit their Tracking Thinking poster paper one more time.	**Why is it important to intentionally plan questions before teaching a lesson?**
Mini-Inquiry 3—Analyzing: Repeat the process using new text examples. After each round of inquiry, be sure to identify a new color of marker for students to update their thinking on their poster. If time (or for groups that finish ahead of time), the process can be repeated. Repeating this process multiple times allows deeper analysis and time for students to notice and synthesize patterns across several sets of paired texts. Students will also be noticing patterns across the work of other groups in the Gallery Walk. **Ideas for comparing subject representation across mediums:** • View the original cartoon versus the Jim Carrey movie *How the Grinch Stole Christmas.* • Watch a video clip portrayal of a current event versus the story of the event in a newspaper. • Listen to a podcast story versus watching it performed. • Observe an artist's painting of a scene or event versus a written description.	**How does the structure of this lesson help ignite students' synergistic thinking and build a bridge to a deeper conceptual understanding?**
Gallery Walk: Arrange student posters around the room. Have students conduct a brief gallery walk looking for patterns in evidence collected across all groups. **Student Refection:** Ask, "What happened to your thinking since **Mini-Inquiry 1**?" and allow groups to look back on their original thinking (what they recorded on their posters in black marker) and to reflect on the process of how their understanding grew and deepened through each inquiry. Encourage groups to pay attention to the new layers of thinking that were added as indicated by each color. Students discuss at their table groups and then share with the class.	

Extended Writing: Ask students think back to their medium comparisons, their findings, and their discussions. "We started class several days ago with a quote by Marshall McLuhan: "The medium is the message." Now that you have had the opportunity to critique how different mediums treat a subject, write a one-to two-page summary of what you think McLuhan meant. Why is what he said in the 60s still relevant and important to understand today? How will this quote affect the choices you make as an author? Cite specific evidence from your work throughout the week to support your thinking and conclude your writing with a statement that expresses the relationship among *medium, author's purpose* and *subject representation* according to the generalization criteria we have practiced and learned previously: 'I understand that . . .'"	Scaffold writing with graphic organizers and sentence stems Ask questions, based on individual student need, to help uncover patterns or to continue to deepen conceptual understanding.
Lesson Closing Closing question: Ask: *Can one medium be relied on more than another to accurately represent a subject?* (Students Think-Pair-Share their opinions) Create a connection between this lesson and what is coming next.	**How can the lesson closing be used to deepen or extend conceptual understanding?**

Materials/Resources

- Poster paper for each group
- Set of colored markers for each group
- Different mediums of the same subject

Assessment:

- Observation of students' reflections on the Tracking Thinking Charts. Observe how their thinking grew and deepened over the course of the lesson. The intentional use of colors makes this easy to do. [This is also serves as a self-assessment for students.]
- Grade each student's Extended Writing piece.
- Observations of group work.

TABLE 3.4 VERTICAL PROGRESSION FOR MODEL LESSON 3

	Grade 5	Grade 7	Grade 9/10
Generalization (Critiquing Strand)	*Analyzing features in different types of text (print versus digital) enhances a reader's understanding and appreciation of a text.*	*Reading a text before hearing and/or seeing it performed supports a closer analysis of each medium.*	*An author's purpose, audience, and message direct the best choice of communication medium.*

that their knowledge, skills, and understandings (generalizations) are becoming building blocks to learning expectations that lie ahead and that their understandings are becoming more sophisticated and precise each year. This is how we help students develop as capable readers, writers, speakers, presenters, and thinkers!

Model Lesson Plan 4 (drawn from Resource A-6): Producing Text

Introduction

In a unit titled *Personal Narratives: Here's My Story*! fifth-grade students are learning about the elements of a personal narrative. Several examples of personal narratives serve as mentor texts to help students notice how authors craft their narratives so readers can truly imagine being in the event. Many fifth graders struggle to convey events in their writing precisely. Weak description, and too many adjectives contribute to lackluster narratives. In this lesson, students explore the relationship between sharing an event precisely and creating images for a reader. Before having students explore an intentionally designed personal narrative text-set through a Gallery Walk, the teacher conducts a Think-Aloud to model how she knows when a text *shows* versus *tells*. This gives all students access to expert thinking before beginning their mini-inquiry with a partner.

SPOTLIGHT:
High-Impact Literacy Practice #4

Think-Aloud
"When teachers explain their thinking in a way that students can understand, students are better able to imitate the thinking of their teachers. We're not looking for students to simply replicate the work of the teacher but rather to explore the ways that other people think. Thinking is invisible, so teachers have to talk about their thinking. By listening to a teacher think, students are guided through the same cognitive processes that the expert uses, as if they were apprentices" (Fisher, Frey, Hattie, & Thayre, 2017, p. 53).

Things to Notice as You Read Model Lesson Plan 4

- How the teacher intentionally designed a text-set to help students notice patterns across many examples of personal narratives.
- How the teacher held a Think-Aloud to model the thinking process to be used in the Gallery Walk to ensure all students had access to expert thinking.
- How the Gallery Walk structure supports the process of inductive inquiry to promote student-led dialogic learning and to develop conceptual understanding about the writing process.

Reflection on Model Lesson Plan 4

The fourth Model Lesson focuses on the Strand *Producing Text* to help students move from mastering routine writing skills to creating a deep understanding of the choices that writers make to effectively communicate ideas. In this model lesson, if the teacher were to tell her students that they had to analyze four to six different texts, she would have likely have heard a series of moans and groans. It doesn't sound like much fun, does it? However, when it is framed as an investigation into how writers bring events and experiences to life for the reader with the freedom to explore the texts around the room, engagement levels soar. Students are given choice, movement, and the chance to discover understanding on their own. Learning experiences such as Think-Alouds and Gallery Walks help build a conceptual understanding with which students can anchor the new skills they are learning.

Vertical Progressions Support Coherence

Let's think again about the relationship between precise language and creating images in readers' minds. In kindergarten, students may share stories through drawing a picture with labels to focus attention on specific details. By third grade, students demonstrate a greater understanding by conveying experiences in narratives through crafting *descriptions* of actions, thoughts, and feelings. In order to increase depth of understanding through the grade levels, the macroconcepts need to be drilled down to the more specific microconcepts. The more micro (specific) the concept is, the more expertise it takes to understand and express the idea. In other words, a progression of Concept-Based Curriculum units builds depth of understanding as concepts become more exact. Think about this: what separates a novice from an expert in a discipline? It's the understanding of the microconcepts and the precise knowledge of the qualities unique to the subject.

In the vertical progression for students learning about precise language (see Table 3.5 on page 56), notice the nuances in microconcepts that separate the fifth-grade generalization from the eighth- and ninth/tenth-grade generalizations. Do you see how the expectations for students' understanding become more sophisticated and exact through the grades?

FIGURE 3.8 MODEL LESSON PLAN 4

CONCEPT-BASED MODEL LESSON 4

Unit Title: *Personal Narratives: Here's My Story*
Grade Level: 5 **Lesson Time Frame**: 2–3 days

Lesson Opening: (to be communicated with students at lesson onset)

In this unit, we've been thinking a lot about our experiences. Sometimes things happen in our lives that make us feel sad, other times we are presented with challenges to overcome, and of course we have many happy memories too. We have so much to share with each other! As fifth-grade students, you are becoming more mature in your writing. We are starting to realize that adding more adjectives does not always make our writing more descriptive.

Over the course of the next couple days, we are going to investigate how writers bring events and experiences to life for the reader. Our inquiry goal is for you to deepen your understanding of how writers effectively craft personal narratives. You can use what you learn from other authors to better share your own story in your own personal narrative collection.

To begin, I'd like to share with you two stories. I'm interested to see what you notice about the similarities and differences between the way the author shares what happened to her!

Learning Targets: What students will Understand (Generalizations), Know and be able to Do (Skills)

Generalization(s) (Students will understand that . . .) Note: Generalizations may apply to one or a series of lessons. G# indicates the target generalization from the curriculum unit.

Unit G#5:) Writers create precise images of people, places, and events in a reader's mind through specific words and details.

5a. What do you notice about how__(author) described the people, places, and events in your story? (F)
5b. What does it mean for a writer to show vs. tell? (F)
5c. How did the author of your book appeal to readers' senses? (F)
5d. How does an author's word choice create images for readers? (C)
5e. How does a personal narrative make it easier for a writer to create precise images for readers? (C)

Strand	Critical Content (Know)	Key Skills (Able to Do)
Understanding Text	• Story elements: character, plot, setting, conflict, events, and so on • Inference	CCSS.ELA-LITERACY.RL.5.1: Quote accurately from a text when explaining what the text says explicitly and when drawing inferences from the text.
Responding to Text	• Questions to clarify, fortify, extend • Strategies for active listening	CCSS.ELA-LITERACY.SL.5.1C: Pose and respond to specific questions by making comments that contribute to the discussion and elaborate on the remarks of others.
Critiquing Text	• Elements of personal narratives	CCSS.ELA-LITERACY. RL.5.2: Compare and contrast stories in the same genre (for example, mysteries and adventure stories) on their approaches to similar themes and topics.
Producing Text	• Definition of precise language, concrete words and phrases, and sensory details	CCSS.ELA-LITERACY.W.5.3D: Use concrete words and phrases and sensory details to convey experiences and events precisely.

(Continued)

FIGURE 3.8 (Continued)

Learning Experiences	Differentiation
Hook: Share an excerpt from a personal narrative that *tells* about an experience through vague descriptions and weak adjectives, such as the example below: *I got stuck and freaked out. I didn't know what to do.* Ask GQ#5a. *What do you notice about how________ (author) described the event in the story? (F)* Students share what they noticed. Share a short personal narrative that precisely *shows* the reader an experience using concrete words and phrases, and sensory details, such as the example below: *Pulling with all my might, I frantically tried to dislodge myself from the barbed wire fence. I knew my mother would be sick with worry over the late hour, but I was coming to realize that my efforts to free my jeans from the wires were futile. I had two choices—leave the new birthday gift on the fence or face humiliation when the sunlight brought the other children walking past old farmer John's field.* Ask GQ#5a. *What do you notice about how________ (author) described the event in the story? (F)* Students share what they noticed. *Ask students which version they liked better. Why? What made the difference between the two? Were they about the same topic?* Ask GQ# 5b. *Based on want you noticed in the two stories, what does it mean to show vs. tell? (F) What does "showing" do for the reader?* [creates images and so on] *Can you better "see" the event in the second example?* Inform students that they *are going to investigate how writers of personal narratives use specific words and details to "show" vs. tell their readers about people, places, and/or events.* *Let students know that through* the learning experiences ahead they should think about the relationship between an author's *specific words and details* and a reader's *mental images.*	**How does the lesson opening and hook immediately engage students' minds and interests?**
Think-Aloud: Think-Aloud to model an explanation of how and why a text *shows* vs. *tells.* Think-Aloud Steps: **Name the strategy, or skill:** *As I am reading this narrative, I can tell that the experience described precisely because the writer shows . . .* **Explain when the strategy or skill is used:** *When the text says____ (quote/detail) it appeals to my senses by helping me:* • *see . . .because . . .* • *feel . . . because . . .* • *hear . . . because . . .* • *think of ___ smell . . . because . . .* **Explain how or why the strategy or skill is used:** *I think the author uses details like______ (quote) so that as the reader I can . . .* Repeat this process using a text that does not *show*, drawing attention to why the text is lacking. Explain that students should talk through the process of explaining *why* a text does or does not precisely *show* the reader the people, places, and events in the examples (as modeled in the Think-Aloud) when they explore the personal narratives with their partner in the Gallery Walk. Let students know you will be listening in and observing active listening and for how they pose questions to each other that extend, clarify, or fortify thinking. (If necessary, briefly review the criteria of each type of question from a previously constructed class anchor chart)	Distribute the sentence stems modeled during the Think-Aloud to support and extend students' academic language development throughout the remainder of lesson. **How does learning through an intentionally designed personal narrative text-set with a gallery walk allow students to cognitively wrestle with and synthesize the knowledge, skills, and concepts under study?**
Mini-inquiry Structured as a Gallery Walk: Create a text-set of excerpts from personal narratives designed to lead students to unit generalization #5. Most text examples should demonstrate how *Personal narratives create images of people, places, and events in a reader's mind precisely through specific words and details*, but a few of the texts can be non-examples. (Seeing non-examples helps students solidify their understanding of the examples as they notice attributes that are missing.)	

Post the text-set across six to eight exhibits, or stations around the room. Students travel with partners, visiting each exhibit. As they visit each exhibit, students analyze and discuss the posted texts. Students complete a graphic organizer featuring guiding questions to help organize and scaffold thinking. On the graphic organizer, students should quote accurately, analyze the quote, and reflect on the choices of the author. **Guiding Questions on the Graphic Organizer:** 1. What details (quotes) in the text seem to *show* the reader the people, places and events in the experience in vivid, realistic ways? 2. How does the detail(s) appeal to your senses? 3. Why do you think the author chose to include that detail? (F)	Provide texts that represent a range of interests and reading levels. Create a graphic organizer using the guiding questions to scaffold thinking.
Notice Patterns: At the end of the gallery walk, ask student groups to first reflect on their work in the Gallery Walk. Next, students Think, Pair, then Share responses to GQ#5c–e with class: 5c. How did the authors appeal to readers' senses? (F) 5d. How did the authors' word choice create images for readers? (C) 5e. How does a personal narrative make it easier for a writer to create precise images for readers? (C) Create a list of on the board as students report out answers so they can begin to look for patterns.	**In this learning experience, what is the role of the teacher? What is the role of the student? Who is responsible for the construction of meaning?**
Pause & Zoom-in: Refer back to the patterns noticed/discussed and ask: What is the definition of precise language? What are concrete words and phrases? What are sensory details? How do we use these techniques in our writing? Conduct a minilesson to develop the skill of using concrete words and phrases and sensory details to convey experiences and events precisely. **Teacher Model:** Teacher takes a vague sentence describing a personal experience, and Thinks Aloud the revision process with the class. The teacher defines each technique and models how to use concrete words and sensory details to convey what the people and the places in the experience look like, sound like, feel like, smell like, and so on. The revised version should convey the experience precisely. **Guided Practice:** In pairs, with feedback and support from the teacher, students experiment with describing common scenes from school, such as eating lunch in the cafeteria, forgetting an important homework assignment at home, getting a strong mark on a challenging test, or playing an intense game of four-square at recess. The school scenes can be shared as a class. Students should reflect on the specific words and details and how precise language appeals to your senses.	**How does noticing patterns across many examples develop conceptual understanding?** **How is this different from focusing instruction on one text?** Deliver additional instruction to individuals or small groups of students based on need. Structure collaborative groups to support the needs of diverse learners.
Independent Practice and Author's Craft Report: Ask students to write about a personal experience by describing a time in which they felt a strong emotion. After they complete their written piece, students write a brief "Craft Report" responding to the prompt: "In a short paragraph, cite examples of the specific words and sensory details you included in your written piece to create more precise mental images for your readers." Ask students to reflect on their process and product and set individual writing goals. Teacher assesses the writing samples to determine areas of need for future writing mini-lessons	**Throughout this lesson plan, how does the teacher show a deliberate effort to use questions to help students bridge from the factual to the conceptual level of thinking?**
Lesson Closing Explain that through the Think-Aloud, Gallery Walk and the writing minilesson, students developed and demonstrated a deeper understanding of how the genre of personal narratives effectively create precise images in a reader's mind. Now, we are ready to begin crafting an extended personal narrative to be included in *Personal Narratives: Here's My Story* collection. In the next lesson, students will begin considering potential memories to write about through a structured brainstorming protocol.	

(Continued)

FIGURE 3.8 (Continued)

Materials/Resources:

- Single-genre set of excerpts, examples and non-examples, from personal narratives designed to lead students to the understanding in the generalization.
- Graphic organizer to help students organize thinking during the Gallery Walk.
- Excerpt from a personal narrative to use for a teacher-led Think-Aloud. The excerpt should provide a clear example of showing vs. telling.
- Sticky notes

Assessment:

- Observations during the Gallery Walk.
- Completed graphic organizers during the Gallery Walk.
- Observations during the minilesson, guided practice, and independent practice
- Assessment of the practice writing tasks to determine the focus of future writing mini-lessons
- Student self-assessment and individually set writing goals
- Understanding of the target generalization in craft report

Why is it important to assess using a variety of assessment methods in authentic contexts?

TABLE 3.5 VERTICAL PROGRESSION FOR MODEL LESSON 4

	Grade 5	Grade 8	Grade 9/10
Generalization (Producing Strand)	*Writers create precise images of people, places, and events in a reader's mind through specific words and details.*	*Writers capture action and convey experiences and events through use of precise words and phrases, relevant descriptive details, and sensory language that pull readers into the plot of a story.*	*Writers create vivid pictures of the experiences, events, setting, and characters of a story through precise words and phrases, telling details, and sensory language that provide the reader with insights into the theme of the story.*

Summary

By the time students enter fourth grade, they have had years of reading instruction and practice. This doesn't mean they have outgrown specific instruction about the reading process. In fact, the amount of independent reading in increasingly complex texts is rapidly rising for students, and too often this is when they begin a downward spiral in their learning. As you design your own Concept-Based literacy lessons, refer back to this chapter often. The four lesson plans in this chapter are here for you to analyze, imitate, and use as inspiration as you design learning for your unique students. We are now ready for Chapter 4, where we help you think about how to design the learning experiences within a lesson plan so that conceptual understanding is continuously deepened.

Extending Thought

The question boxes embedded throughout each Model Lesson are intended to extend your thinking and provoke discussions with colleagues.

Remember: "All progress takes place outside the comfort zone." —Michael John Bobak

CHAPTER 4

Designing Learning Experiences That Develop Conceptual Understanding

FIGURE 4.1

As literacy teachers, we love to read. We are constantly on the lookout for engaging texts to capture the hearts and minds of our students and for professional resources featuring new practices to add to our instructional repertoires. We gather a few ideas from one resource and a few from another, or maybe a colleague down the hall shares a great activity. After several years of collecting, our files are overflowing! So much so that sometimes it is hard to know what learning experience to use when, and which learning experiences are most effective.

In this chapter, we give closer attention to the types of student learning experiences assigned in Concept-Based classrooms. Learning experiences are the activities, work, or tasks where students practice relevant literacy skills, grapple with complex situations, collaborate with peers, and develop their conceptual thinking. Different learning experiences require different levels of student engagement. When tasks require students to be actively engaged, we

Teaching to a conceptual level of understanding does not mean that all your "old" literacy learning experiences are no longer relevant or valued. Many of your current practices are still useful in developing what students will Know, Understand, and be able to Do.

know the learning will be more memorable and enjoyable. However, we also want to make sure that the learning experiences we assign deliberately cultivate students' conceptual minds if we are to support the transfer of understanding.

Teaching to a conceptual level of understanding does not mean that all your "old" literacy learning experiences are no longer relevant or valued. Many of your current practices are still useful in developing what students will **K**now, **U**nderstand, and be able to **D**o. This chapter showcases familiar literacy learning experiences that go beyond to deliberately leverage students' *conceptual understanding* of what it takes to be a capable reader, writer, viewer, speaker, listener, presenter, and researcher.

Moving Beyond Skills to Conceptual Understanding That Transfers

Academic standards define the grade-level benchmarks students are expected to meet in various subject areas. When you look at standards for English, it becomes evident that literacy is a discipline organized primarily by the processes, strategies, and skills students are expected to be able to **D**o. However, teaching students the strategies and skills within processes is not the end goal. Moving student learning beyond practicing strategies and skills to deeper conceptual understandings develops disciplinary expertise and better enables students to transfer complex skills to new situations. Small-group discourse, for example, is worthier of our students' time if it leads to new capabilities, knowledge, and understandings about the discourse process. Too often we concentrate on students' learning skills or strategies but stop short of making sure our students *understand and can transfer* their learning. The result is a never-ending cycle of "What skill are we going to *cover* next?" without time to pause and plan how that skill will transfer to learning expectations ahead or to life outside of school.

Moving student learning beyond practicing strategies and skills to deeper conceptual understandings develops disciplinary expertise and better enables students to transfer complex skills to new situations.

In three-dimensional Concept-Based Curriculum and Instruction, we teach literacy skills and strategies within the context of well-thought-out, sequential instructional units and lessons that intentionally develop a third dimension—students' conceptual schemata. In other words, students learn and practice skills in contexts that support inquiry and exemplify the relationships among the specific skills and related concepts. Conceptual understanding brings relevance to literacy learning.

Sometimes Conceptual Understanding Is Inadvertently Shortchanged . . .

Take a peek at this example from a fourth-grade classroom:

The students in this fourth-grade classroom are fired up! While learning about the concept of conservation in science, the students discovered that many people in their school waste a lot of food. During a food waste audit, which was one of the learning experiences in the fourth-grade science unit, the students discovered uneaten sandwiches, apples without a bite taken, unopened sticks of string cheeses, and mounds of food from the hot lunch served that day. The fourth graders were shocked at just how much edible food is thrown away, even though the school recently conducted a food drive to help combat hunger in their community. Three-dimensional instruction in the Concept-Based science curriculum unit moved student learning beyond knowing the meaning of conservation to a deeper, transferable generalization: "Food waste undermines conservation efforts and perpetuates needless hunger."

By the end of the unit, students were feeling inspired to bring about change. They asked the teacher what they could do to let others in the school know how much food is being wasted. The teacher quickly recognized how he could use the students' science learning as a perfect vehicle for integrating some of the English language arts presentation skills and the technology skills that are also part of the fourth-grade curricula.

In his next lesson, the teacher asks students to collaboratively create a PowerPoint presentation so they can share what they learned about food waste. They will present their findings to classrooms across the school. This activity will integrate science, literacy, and technology as students present to an authentic audience. Perfect!

TABLE 4.1 TWO-DIMENSIONAL LITERACY LEARNING EXPECTATIONS FROM A GRADE 4 CLASSROOM EXAMPLE

2-Dimensional Learning Expectations (facts & skills)	Content in the students' PowerPoint presentation will demonstrate students ***K**now* . . . • The meaning of conservation • Relevant facts about a topic from research Key Skills students will be able to ***D**o* . . . • Report on the topic in an organized manner • Pose and respond to specific questions to clarify or follow up on information, and make comments that contribute to the discussion and link to the remarks of others • Build a digital presentation with a focus on skill development, such as ◦ Inserting images into a presentation ◦ Using bulleted lists to organize ideas ◦ Selecting color scheme ◦ Using appropriate font size and style . . . but what will students ***U**nderstand*?

Let's pause here for a moment. Although the students are highly engaged and motivated about creating their presentations, there is a problem. Do the expectations in Table 4.1 represent three-dimensional learning? In fact, the learning expectations reflect two-dimensional learning. They are all at the factual and skill levels. Yes, the teacher guided the students to an important science generalization, but in terms of skill instruction, what transferable, conceptual understanding will students uncover about effective presentations? It is easy to insert literacy skill expectations into content lessons without realizing that students' learning may fall short of conceptual understanding. Important skills require three-dimensional teaching as well. The learning expectations in Table 4.1 never rise above facts and skills to conceptual understanding.

How can this fourth-grade teacher move students' learning to a conceptual level? He first needs to identify a clear learning target of conceptual understanding (generalization) by asking, "What do I want my students to *Understand* about presentation skills as a result of this learning experience? What is it that students need to *Understand* in order to apply the skills they are learning to new and more novel situations?" If the teacher selects the generalization, *Authors choose a presentation style and visuals that effectively convey key points to a target audience*, as his focus for instruction, can you begin to see how he could redesign the learning experience to deliberately guide students to this conceptual understanding? As a result, conceptual understanding would not be shortchanged.

Developing Three-Dimensional Learning Experiences

The ultimate goal is that students can use language to *articulate* what they are thinking and understanding as a result of their experiences.

Practicing skills that are locked into a specific assignment does not necessarily result in learning transfer—especially when the new context is unfamiliar and more complex.

We know that practicing skills that are locked into a specific assignment does not necessarily lead to learning transfer—especially when the new context is unfamiliar and more complex. When we begin thinking like a three-dimensional teacher, first and foremost, we consider the literacy learner. In other words, by the end of the lesson(s), we want our learners to have a deeper understanding of how "literacy works." Attention is given not only to how well a student demonstrates proficiency with a particular skill in a specific situation. The ultimate goal is that students can use language to *articulate* what they are thinking and understanding as a result of their experiences. Language is central to learning. Language makes it possible to cognitively reconstruct the experience and in doing so, clarify, share, internalize, and ultimately transfer the learning. Teaching skills is not the end goal in and of itself. Rather, the skills are taught to exemplify a bigger idea or a target generalization. When we take our thinking about how to teach complex skills and knowledge one step further, we are better able to make conscious choices about literacy practices that will deliberately guide students' thinking toward the realization of target generalizations.

Snapshots of Concept-Based Literacy Classrooms

The remainder of this chapter lists Snapshots of CBCI classrooms showcasing learning experiences that cultivate students' conceptual minds and support transfer. The different Snapshots paint pictures of how we engage synergistic thinking, support the process of inquiry, and help students move from the practice of a concrete skill or example to a deeper conceptual understanding about the reading, writing, speaking, and listening processes. Many of the approaches are most likely already in your instructional toolbox, but notice how these examples push beyond and continuously develop students' conceptual schema.

Things to look for as you browse the Snapshots:

- How generalizations are used as instructional targets
- How the teacher uses a conceptual lens to direct student thinking
- How students notice patterns across multiple texts
- How the teacher uses instructional techniques familiar to many literacy classrooms
- How student reflection is valued
- How students are brought to uncover the generalization

Not all Snapshot examples incorporate each of the items mentioned above, nor does every Snapshot require students to demonstrate transfer as some of the lessons are at different points along that path to uncovering a generalization. We hope the breadth of examples (you might not want to read them all at once!) will spark ideas for your classroom as you continue to refine your journey as a CBCI teacher.

Considering Familiar Practices Through a Concept-Based Literacy Design Framework

Familiar Practices Showcased in the Classroom Snapshots:

- Beginning With a Hook
- Entrance Ticket
- Anticipation Guide
- Mentor Texts
- Think-Aloud
- Teacher Modeling
- Minilesson
- Writer's Workshop
- Writer's Conference
- Building Anchor Charts
- Sentence Stems
- Metacognition
- Close Reading
  - Repeated Reading
  - Annotating Texts
- Strategic Questioning
- Comprehension Strategies
  - Summarizing
  - Self-Regulating
  - Creating Meaningful Connections
  - Inferring
- Student Reflection
- Collaborative Learning
- Explicit Instruction
- Independent Practice
- Written Conversation
- Artifact Box
- Co-creation of Rubrics
- Sorting Examples
- Scaffolding Thinking With Graphic Organizers
- Reading Across Documents
- Single-genre Text Set
- Multi-genre Text Set
- Independent Reading at Home
- Academic Conversations
- Gallery Walk
- Student-led Dialogic Learning
  - Partner Discussions
  - Small-Group Discussions
  - Socratic Seminar
- Short Research Project
- Craft Report
- Low-Risk Writing
- Extended Writing
- Morning Meeting
- Think Pair Share
- Ranking Concepts
- Sorting Concepts
- Exit Slips
- Sticky Note Reflection
- I Can Statements

Types of Texts Showcased in the Classroom Snapshots:

- Short stories
- Novels
- Informational Texts
- Poetry
- Spoken Word Poetry Performance
- Graphic Novels
- Artwork
- Photographs
- Podcasts
- Sentence Examples
- Student Work Samples

Concept-Based Literacy takes your familiar learning practices one step further, so they deliberately leverage students' conceptual understanding of what it takes to be a capable reader, writer, viewer, speaker, listener, presenter, and researcher.

CONCEPT-BASED CLASSROOM SNAPSHOT 1

Concept Cards

Sixth-grade students are exploring the genre of fantasy in a unit titled "Other Worlds, Magic, and Creatures, Oh My!" The duel conceptual lens of the unit is *Literary Analysis/Argumentation*. Up to this point, students analyzed various narrative elements and identified themes in their novels. The teacher knows that a summary paragraph, something students have learned to write in the past, will not be sufficient. It is time to introduce the skill of writing longer sustained analysis essays in a way that will engage students' conceptual minds.

The teacher wants students to first investigate the differences between more concise summaries and elements of extended arguments. Before becoming a Concept-Based teacher, she may have listed the steps to writing an argument for students (for example, make a claim, organize reasoning, support the claim with specific passages from the text that tie to other moments in the book). Now she turns the thinking over to her students using Concept Cards that capture microconcepts related to the unit's conceptual lens.

Concept-Based Students use conceptual language confidently and accurately.

1. The teacher distributes an example of a literary analysis paragraph (summary) and an example of a longer literary analysis essay (argument). Both represent the same text.
2. The teacher hands out a packet of Concept Cards. She asks students to pull out the card labeled *Claim and asks, "What do you notice about how each example presents a Claim?"* Students discuss in pairs and share out as a class.
3. The teacher asks students to find the card Text Structure and to examine the two examples using the question, "*How is the Text Structure the same or different in the text examples?*" Students discuss in pairs and share out as a class.
4. Students make the same comparison with the remaining two Concept Cards labeled *Evidence* and *Writing Style*.

Through this process, students linked a concept, critical to writing an effective argument, to a concrete example. Synergistic thinking was ignited as students were invited to process factual information through the different concepts.

It is the interplay between the lower and higher levels of thinking that leads to deeper understanding and transfer. Concept Cards are similar to a Conceptual Lens (where teachers use a macro or broad concept to identify a unit focus); the concepts on the Concept Cards direct and focus students' thinking. The difference is that Concept Cards use concepts that are more micro (specific), relevant to the particular learning experience, and related to the conceptual focus of the unit.

Notice how thinking shifts when viewing an example through one concept and then another.

To make the cards, identify the important concepts under study, and write one concept per card. If possible, laminate the cards to ensure durability for frequent use.

CONCEPT-BASED CLASSROOM SNAPSHOT 2

Lesson Openings

Each day, seventh-grade students begin their class by engaging in entry tasks and activities that tap their prior knowledge, engage synergistic thinking, and cultivate curiosity. The teacher intentionally designs her lesson openings to capture students' attention by sharing intriguing images, insightful quotes, or conceptual questions, but she doesn't stop there. She gives students the challenge of thinking about the new learning through the unit's conceptual lens, or a related microconcept critical to the upcoming lesson. In the examples below, notice how the opening hook in each of the three examples, from different units, ignites synergistic thinking.

After sharing a quote, students view the quote through the unit's conceptual lens, which is critical to the upcoming lesson.

Conceptual Lens: Point of View

You never really understand a person until you consider things from his point of view—until you climb into his skin and walk around in it."

—Harper Lee

How does this quote help you better understand the meaning point of *view*?

Concept-Based Students develop the mental models and conceptual schema needed to retrieve when trying to make sense of new knowledge.

At the lesson opening, students are asked to use what they currently understand about a familiar macroconcept (*text analysis*) as they complete an anticipation guide and contemplate more microconcepts that are important to the upcoming lesson.

Deep Text Analysis vs. Surface Text Analysis

Based on what you know right now, what are the characteristics of each type of analysis?

Deep Text Analysis	Surface Text Analysis

The first lesson of this unit opens with a debatable question about the unit's conceptual lens to activate synergistic thinking.

Conceptual Lens: Bias

Is it possible to completely rid yourself of bias?

CONCEPT-BASED CLASSROOM SNAPSHOT 3

Think-Alouds

As fourth-grade students explore the genre of poetry in a unit titled "Poets' Purposeful Word Play," with a conceptual lens *Inference*, they are learning how authors leave clues in texts that require readers to infer. In this lesson, the teacher targets the unit generalization, *Readers make inferences by combining information from their background knowledge with details from a text to uncover deeper meaning.*

As a first step in guiding students to this generalization, the teacher uses a Think-Aloud to show how she makes inferences based on the author's use of sensory details in poetry. Creating an interplay between the students' factual and conceptual levels of thinking ignites synergistic thinking. Subsequent lessons will help students notice patterns across emerging examples that reflect the generalization.

Excerpt From the Think-Aloud

Teacher:

"As I read this poem, I'm wondering what can we infer or understand about the author's feelings?"

"Hmm . . . Let me see . . . . I can infer that she is very sad and crying. She wishes she had a dog to hug, but I don't think that she is crying because she wants a dog. Something else is making her sad."

"The author helped me understand that she was sad by giving me some clues. She said that her eyes were red and puffy, her nose was sniffly, and that there was salt on her cheeks. Those are all sensory details, right?"

"When I read this it makes me feel sad with her. I'm wondering, would I, as the reader, feel this sadness with the author had she simply said "I am sad" rather than using the sensory details that she used? I don't think so, but I'm not really sure why. Now that makes me wonder, why do readers more deeply understand a text when the author describes emotions using sensory details?"

"Class, why does it seem to be more effective for the author to convey feelings through those sensory details rather than just saying it in a straightforward way?"

Luis:

"I think it is because the words helped me SEE her. It reminded me of the time my little brother dropped his piggy bank and it shattered everywhere. He cried so much that his eyes were super puffy and his nose wouldn't stop running. I felt bad for him. I think that must be how the author felt."

Teacher:

"Thank you, Luis. You connected your background knowledge to the sensory details! As you explore the other poems located around the room over the next couple of days, pay attention to how the authors communicate emotions using sensory details that require the reader to make inferences. Select three poems to read closely. Record what you notice about the author's use of sensory details on your graphic organizer by answering questions 1-4 (below)."

Concept-Based Students independently link factual examples to related concepts and generalizations.

Poem Title and Author	1) What can you infer about how the author/ narrator of the poem was feeling? (F)	2) What sensory detail gave you a clue about how the author/ narrator was feeling? (F)	3) How did your background knowledge help you make this inference? (F)	4) What else did you do as a reader to make the inference? (F)

Students complete the task over a couple of days, and the teacher then asks the class to consider the information they collected as they respond to the following questions: "What happens when readers do not make inferences?(C) How does inferring help readers uncover a deeper meaning of the text?" (C)

In this Think-Aloud, the teacher modeled the reading strategy of making inferences and designed a task to help students express a generalization about the reading process. Articulating conceptual understanding adds a three-dimensional layer and a conceptual link to previous learning and to learning up ahead.

CONCEPT-BASED CLASSROOM SNAPSHOT 4

Close Reading

In a tenth-grade English class, students are deep in a unit titled "Along the Continuum of Truth and Lie" with the conceptual lens *Argumentation* providing a focus of study. Texts about the food industry provide engaging content for the processes, strategies, and skills students will **K**now, **U**nderstand, and be able to **D**o by the end of the unit. Students are already finding the food industry riddled with conflicting information, bias, and high-dollar advertising, all of which make it challenging to know what to accept as truth. It is a perfect topic to ignite curiosity and prompt inquiry. One student in the class is a vegan, and ready to prove that meat production is destroying our environment. Another student believes dairy is the cause of most of today's health problems. And yet another student thinks a cheeseburger and fries are a fantastic meal. While most students fall somewhere in between, everyone has questions about the way food is produced (industrial, organic, local sustainable, GMO, the list goes on.), what is in our foods (additives, preservatives, artificial vs. natural colors and so forth), and of course, the question of what is healthy and what is not. This case study becomes personally meaningful and relevant three times a day. However, because this is an English class, the teacher knows she must deliberately address students' conceptual understanding of processes.

During a weeklong mini-inquiry into the relationship between the concepts of *argument*, *evidence*, and *reasoning*, students craft an inquiry question about a debatable topic related to the case study. Students conduct individual research, and based on their findings, form a claim in response to the inquiry question. Students then locate two articles—one in support of their argumentative claim, and one that could be used as evidence against their claim. Next, they analyze each article using the close reading process (below). To ignite synergistic thinking during the process of close reading, students focus on microconcepts drawn from the target generalization. This creates an interplay between the factual and conceptual levels of thinking as students analyze and annotate the articles.

Concept-Based Students bring their own thinking to and make personal meaning of the factual study by viewing learning through a conceptual lens.

Reading	Purpose of Reading	Microconcept	Guiding Question
First	*Delineate the author's argument*	*Claim*	*1. What is the author's claim? (F)* *2. What evidence did the author use to support the claim? (F)*
Second	*Evaluate whether the evidence is relevant and sufficient*	*Evidence*	*3. Was the author's evidence relevant and sufficient? (F)*
Third	*Assess whether the reasoning is valid. Identify fallacious reasoning.*	*Valid Argument*	*4. Was the author's reasoning valid? Support with evidence. (F)*

After the process of close reading, students work in small groups and hold a silent written conversation to discuss guiding questions: *What makes reasoning sound? (C)*, and *What happens when authors use fallacious reasoning? (C)*. Each student answers the two conceptual questions on his or her own paper, and then passes his or her paper to the student to the left. With the new paper in hand, students read the answers written by their classmates, respond in writing to the ideas presented, and ask questions to promote further thinking. They then again pass the paper to the left. Students repeat this process and continue to rotate papers around the group until each student receives his or her original paper back. For the final step, students read the written conversation that occurred on their paper, and discuss pertinent ideas verbally.

To conclude, students answer guiding question, *What is the relationship between argument, evidence, and reasoning?(C)* as they craft generalizations to articulate their understanding of the relationship between the concepts under study.

CONCEPT-BASED CLASSROOM SNAPSHOT 5

Text-Sets

Ninth-grade students are immersed in a Concept-Based Curriculum unit titled "Different Authors, Different Mediums, Telling the Same Story." The unit's conceptual lens is Critical Stance. Students will be studying the fine (blurred or overt) line that exists in the portrayal of an event through different authors and mediums. Author's purpose, themes, techniques, and style are some of the elements that will be compared and analyzed over the course of the unit so that students will learn what goes into making an informed critical stance. The teacher created artifact boxes (folders) containing text-sets. Each text in the artifact box is in a different medium and created by a different author, but all the texts depict the same event. The text-sets will serve different purposes in several of the unit's lessons; some of the texts within a set may change depending on lesson focus.

Concept-Based Students can transfer their learning across multiple types of literary materials and genres.

This lesson spans approximately 2–3 days. The text-sets provide the context for the target curriculum unit generalization: Authors shape and refine characters, conflict, and specific details, which readers use to uncover themes. In small groups, students explore each text in the artifact box and answer answer guiding questions 1–3 on the graphic organizer (below). Through the intentionally designed guiding questions and the multi-genre text-set, students construct meaning on their own through an inductive process. After responding to the questions, students look across the information and construct a theme statement for each text type. They may find the theme changes or remains the same, but they must be able to defend their stance using text evidence.

Text-Set	1) What is happening to the main character/person? (F)	2) What is the conflict? Does the conflict represent a bigger, abstract idea? (F)	3) What details are significant? (F)	4) Express the relationship among the concepts of character, conflict, and details, in a theme statement (generalization). (C)
Written Text (may be more than one type)				
Artwork				
Photograph				
How does exploring a theme of the same event through the eyes of different authors help readers take a more informed stance? (C)				

Notice how the text-set leads students to understandings important to English language arts. The learning experience is designed to engage students in the *reading* and *writing* processes using the text-set content understudy. An example of the texts that might be in an artifact box is below:

Text-Set Topic: American Revolution

- Informational article about Paul Revere
- Poem—*Paul Revere's Ride* by Henry Wadsworth Longfellow
- Painting—*The Midnight Ride of Paul Revere* by Grant Wood

If the lesson were to assess students' comprehension of content knowledge (for example, *What does each text highlight about Paul Revere?*), learning would be locked to the specific situation; transfer would not be supported; and an understanding important to the discipline of English would be missing.

This lesson goes beyond by asking students to uncover text examples of concepts, look for patterns across different mediums, and synthesize the information to construct generalizations that are transferable to other learning situations. Lots of thinking is required and within reach of all students, as long as the readability of the text-set is accessible to the readers.

CONCEPT-BASED CLASSROOM SNAPSHOT 6

Text Case Studies

In a seventh-grade unit titled "Historical Fiction: Going Back in Time Through Literary Travels," students are in the midst of exploring how authors use and alter history when writing fictional narratives by comparing their novel with research from the same time period

Rather than having all students read the same title, each student self-selects a novel from a classroom text-set consisting of a range of historical fiction titles representing diverse eras and perspectives. The process of selecting novels creates a contagious energy in the room, and students are eager to dig in!

The students are ready to investigate the relationship between author's craft and the development of time and place in narratives. The teacher wants students to uncover the generalization, *Authors of historical fiction develop time and place through the use of description, dialogue, and characters' actions that are authentic to the historical era.*

In previous lessons, students selected a scene from their novel and conducted research to locate the actual historical account of the time period. They created a Venn diagram to compare and contrast their novel with their research of the period. Students are now going beyond the collection of facts to identify *how* their author used and altered history in their fictional account.

Concept-Based Students transform examples and ideas into higher-level generalizations.

	My Novel	How is this similar to or different from the historical account? (F)
What do you know about the *time* and *place* of the story from the author's description? (F)		
What do you know about the *time* and *place* of the story from the dialogue? (F)		
What do you know about the *time* and *place* of the story from the actions of the characters? (F)		
How do authors of fiction draw on and alter history to develop time and place in narratives? (C)		

To conclude the inquiry, students work in small groups to answer the question *How do authors of fiction draw on and alter history to develop time and place in narratives?* (C) The class has a range of different texts to help build an understanding of setting, time, and place in narratives, so students can readily share with others and discuss patterns across their examples. On sticky notes, students finish the statement "I understand that . . ." to write a generalization using the literacy concepts and patterns of evidence they uncovered when they discussed their individual case studies.

In the remainder of the unit, students will engage in other mini-inquiries that target different generalizations. Each inquiry will allow students to use their own novel as individual case studies. By providing texts from different time periods and varying lengths and readability levels, students who finish ahead of others can continue to push themselves as readers by moving to another next book. Students who read more slowly are honored by not feeling like they have to "keep up" with the class. The student choice in reading novels and the student voice in sharing their thoughts and findings cultivate learning partnerships and responsibility rather than a reliance on the teacher.

CONCEPT-BASED CLASSROOM SNAPSHOT 7

Independent Novels

Eighth-grade students are using their independent novels to explore the relationship between characters' dialogue and the advancement of action in the plot. The novels provide the context for individual case studies, and although self-selected, teacher guidance assists in matching titles to students' interest and readability levels. Independent reading is assigned each night for 20 minutes as homework. For the past week, students were asked to pay careful attention to the dialogue in their texts and the impact the dialogue had on their story's course of action.

Students begin class by completing an entrance ticket with the following factual guiding questions: What example of dialogue did you highlight in your reading last night? Did that dialogue affect the action of your story in any way? If so, explain. Since students are drawing on specific instances from a specific text, their answers are considered factual examples.

Concept-Based Students express conceptual relationships drawn from factual examples.

At the end of the week, students engage in a Think, Pair, Share discussion about their answers to the guiding questions. After discussion, students ponder the conceptual question, What is the relationship between dialogue and action in a story? Their generalizations are written on sticky notes, which are then placed on a class anchor chart titled "We Understand that . . . (Relationship Between Dialogue and Action)." The following week, students focus their attention how authors use dialogue to reveal aspects of a character.

We understand that . . . *(Relationship Between Dialogue and Action)*	**We understand that . . .** *(Relationship Between Dialogue and Characterization)*

Teaching Idea

Create a space in the room for students to record the information they are uncovering as they use their independent reading novels as case studies.

Rather than just tracking pages or minutes read each night, independent reading novels serve as case studies for a wide range of potential learning. Breaking down complex standards into manageable parts that help students notice patterns representing important concepts maximizes the learning return on the assigned reading. This is a thinking classroom; students will eventually pull their charted information into a broader, more complex generalization. The teacher is deliberately developing students' conceptual schema about the processes important to being a capable reader and writer.

CONCEPT-BASED CLASSROOM SNAPSHOT 8

Mentor Texts

Ninth-grade students are engaged in a unit titled "Famous Speeches, Readings, and Presentations: Speaking so that Audiences Listen," with a conceptual lens *Speaker's Craft*. Throughout the unit, they listen to and view clips of speeches, poetry readings, and presentations by recognized authors and speakers, who serve as mentors, for ways to adapt speech for a variety of contexts and audiences.

In one mini-inquiry, students investigate the relationship between voice (pitch, pause, volume, rhythm, intonation, and so on) and creating an emotional experience for the listener. The teacher is targeting the unit generalization, *Speakers use pitch, pause, volume, rhythm, and intonation to create an emotional experience for the listener.*

After viewing and or listening to clips of poetry performance, students record the traits they believe created an emotional response in themselves—the listener. They support the identified traits with examples from the spoken-word poem.

Concept-Based Students systematically and methodically explain understanding supported by relevant evidence.

Next, students form small collaborative groups to compare evidence. Samples of evidence are written on separate notecards and sorted into categories they title (pitch, pause, volume, and so on).

Finally, the identified categories (concepts) and evidence are shared with the whole group and collapsed onto a class chart. Using the concepts from the chart, students individually craft a generalization as an exit slip from class; "I understand that . . ." The generalizations become the teacher's assessment of students' understanding about the art of spoken-word poetry and may be posted for future reference as the unit work continues.

More ideas for learning from mentor texts

Idea for Using Mentor Texts	Sample Learning Experience
As a writing mentor	Create a text-set of different types of sentences from a piece of mentor text using strips of chart paper. Have students find different ways to sort the sentences according to sentence type or whatever attributes are under study (openings, punctuation, sentence structure, sentence variation, style, formal vs. informal language, and so on)
As a standard to strive for	As a class, construct a rubric from the attributes uncovered in a mentor author's work and have students use the rubric to self-assess their writing or speaking.
As an exemplar to be imitated	*Students may need to first replicate a piece of spoken mentor text before they are ready to recite their own work. This rehearsal provides more support in practicing what it "feels" like to speak well.*

CONCEPT-BASED CLASSROOM SNAPSHOT 9

Gallery Walks

Fourth-grade students are in the midst of of their Concept-Based unit, and the teacher notices extra attention needs to be given to teaching students about the importance of transitional words in writing. This mini-inquiry, which takes place over two blocks of time, Pauses and Zooms in on an exploration of strategies writers use for communicating categories of information clearly.

Before students are expected to use transitional words and phrases as writers, they will investigate the relationship between transitional phrases and a *reader's* understanding of a text. The teacher creates a single genre text-set consisting of samples of writing by fourth-grade students from previous years. Some pieces are well written, effectively using transitional phrases to link ideas (for example, first reason, second reason, because, and so on), while others demonstrate errors common to fourth-grade writers (listing ideas, randomly jumping to new thoughts, and so on). By providing exemplars and non-examples, students are further able to build the schema in their brain.

Concept-Based Students articulate generalizations and provide support with multiple examples.

The teacher divides the text-set across several different exhibits, or stations, to form a gallery in the classroom. In pairs, students travel around the room visiting each exhibit. They analyze and discuss the different texts, responding to questions in the directions in the box below. The questions help students to develop and organize their thinking.

Gallery Walk Directions

With your partner, travel around the room visiting each exhibit.

1. Read the example.
2. Discuss the following questions:
    - Was this paragraph clearly written? (F)
    - Were you able to easily follow the connections between ideas? (F)
    - What do you think made the piece clear or confusing? (F)
3. Note evidence to support your answers for each example.

At the end of the gallery walk, students synthesize their discoveries in small groups and share as a class. The teacher closes the lesson by asking students to reflect on the question, *What is the relationship between a writer's use of transitional phrases and a reader's understanding of a text?* (C) Students collectively craft a generalization on a sticky note by finishing the phrase, "We understand that . . . " to communicate their conceptual understanding. Following this learning experience, students will be writing explanatory paragraphs using transitional phrases to link ideas.

* Note: The difference between a two-dimensional and three-dimensional Gallery Walk is the intended purpose, or instructional target. A three-dimensional Gallery Walk uses an inductive, inquiry-based process to help students discover patterns across several examples that build toward the transferable understanding articulated in the generalization. Through analyzing the characteristics of the examples, students develop a conceptual understanding that is not locked in time, place, situation, or to a specific text or task. The structure of a Gallery Walk is the same in both the 2D and 3D variations, but conceptual understanding is addressed in a 3D version.

CONCEPT-BASED CLASSROOM SNAPSHOT 10

Socratic Seminar

As part of a curriculum unit titled "Short Stories: Weaving a Tapestry of Words" using *Genre* as a conceptual lens, seventh graders are exploring key concepts (character, point of view, setting, conflict, plot, and theme) through a short story genre study. During one mini-inquiry, students analyzed a short story told through multiple points of view to better understand why authors contrast the points of view of different characters in narratives. After experiencing the process of close reading with a short story, the teacher held a Socratic Seminar to allow students to process the short story as a whole class.

After observing the students' level of discourse in the Socratic Seminar, the teacher decides this is a good time to Pause and Zoom in on the process of communication. She wants students to develop a deep understanding of *why* discussion is a critical step in comprehending text. This learning experience (participating in a Socratic Seminar) is part of her instructional sequence, or a means, designed to guide students' thinking to a target generalization from the unit.

To get students to think more deeply about the communication process and their discussion, the teacher asks students to complete a formal reflection using guiding questions (see below). Students work on answering the questions for the remainder of class. The next day, each student writes a generalization expressing the relationship between the *quality of discourse* and a *reader's understanding* of a text. Students finish the statement, "I understand that . . . " and write it in their journal on the page labeled "My Generalizations." Finally, students complete an Exit Slip at the end of class.

Concept-Based Students understand how the skills and strategies they learn are connected to the bigger whole of the authentic inquiry in which they are engaged.

The teacher is now ready to Zoom back out. Students return to investigating key concepts of short stories (content under study). The investigation of the genre was never out of sight for too long. The purpose of taking a moment to pause and reflect on the process of effective communication was to give students more practice with discussion protocols and to develop their understanding of the value of holding such conversations.

Socratic Seminar Reflection

Answer the following questions before beginning your paragraph about the article we discussed.

1. What did you understand about the topic before the discussion? (F)
2. What did someone say during the Socratic Seminar that caused you to think differently about the topic? (F)
3. What role does discourse play in understanding a text? (C)
4. Why is it necessary to revise thinking? (C)
5. Do we always have to accept the ideas of others? (D)

Exit Slip

- How did our discussion protocols contribute to the overall success of your group's conversation? (F)
- How can a discussion with others help keep impulsive decisions in check? (C)

CONCEPT-BASED CLASSROOM SNAPSHOT 11

Reading to Write

In a Concept-Based Curriculum unit titled "Getting to Know Characters," with a conceptual lens of *Character Traits*, fifth-grade students are thinking about how they, as readers, come to know a story's characters. During a previous lesson, a class chart of positive and negative personality traits was brainstormed. Students related many of the traits listed to people they know or to characters they have encountered in their reading.

The teacher now wants students to use the different stories that each small group is reading to think about the different ways an author reveals a character's traits. Students will later use this understanding to improve how they reveal characters in the stories they are working on in their individual process writing folders.

Concept-Based Students understand concepts that show the reciprocal nature of the reading and writing process.

First, the teacher constructs a graphic organizer, such as the example below, and asks student groups to record evidence of how their author revealed the traits of the main character of their story through the character's words, actions, motives, thoughts, and/or relationships with other characters. Once groups finish their text analyses, they share their findings with the class. The teacher captures their information and facilitates the completion of a large class graphic organizer.

Students are now asked to look across the organizer and synthesize the information collected. The teacher asks, *"What do you notice about the different ways authors helped readers learn about a main character?"* (C) One thing students notice is that not every author used every perspective to reveal his/her character. The teacher asks students to go back into their texts and consider, *"Why do you think your author may or may not have addressed every view of your character?"* (F) She moves from group to group providing scaffolding through guiding questions as students grapple with the question. Students conclude that not every author needs to show a character from every perspective because there was already enough information, some information was more explicitly stated, the author wanted the reader to figure things out, and so on.

Finally, the lesson closes with the teacher reinforcing all the hard work and thinking the students did and asks, *"What understanding will you now use when you go back into your process writing folders and continue working on revealing the traits of one of your main characters for your readers? Let's complete the statement, We understand that . . . "* The teacher posts the generalization on the bulletin board titled "Our Generalizations" for future reference.

How Do Authors Reveal a Character's Traits?

What trait(s) best describe your character? (F)	Character's words (page #)	Character's actions (page #)	Character's motives (page #)	Character's thoughts (page #)	Character's relationships with others (page #)

CONCEPT-BASED CLASSROOM SNAPSHOT 12

Craft Report

Tenth-grade students are deep into a Concept-Based Curriculum unit titled "Take A Stance: Constructing Arguments that Prevail," with a conceptual lens *Argumentation*. Students investigated various global debatable issues and are ready to take a stance. To communicate their stance on the issue of their choice, students construct an extended essay demonstrating their skill at constructing arguments.

In the essay, students were expected to:

- Introduce precise claim(s), distinguish the claim(s) from alternate or opposing claims, and create an organization that establishes clear relationships among claim(s), counterclaims, reasons, and evidence. (CCSS.ELA-LITERACY.W.9-10.1.A)
- Develop claim(s) and counterclaims fairly, supplying evidence for each while pointing out the strengths and limitations of both in a manner that anticipates the audience's knowledge level and concerns. (CCSS.ELA-LITERACY.W.9-10.1.B)

The work doesn't stop with the essay, however. The teacher wants to take students another step to be assured they reached the targeted transferable, conceptual understanding about elements of effective arguments, *Effective arguments rely on a precise claim, valid and relevant evidence to support reasoning, and an awareness of audience.* If the teacher's assessment stopped at grading students' essays, he would be assuming understanding is intact. A Craft Report asks students to explain the process they engaged in as writers constructing their argument. Students articulate the specific techniques they used and then explain why the techniques were effective. Students cite specific examples from their essay as evidence.

Concept-Based Students explain the choices they make while engaged in a process and explain why those choices are effective.

Do you see how a Craft Report pushes student thinking beyond mastery of the skills to articulating an understanding of the choices they made as a writers? Craft Reports end with students finishing the statement, "As a result of this study, I understand that . . ."

Sample Craft Report

Craft Move—What did you do as a writer? (F)	Example from your Essay	Why was this choice effective? (C)
As a result of this study, I understand that ? . . . (write a one-sentence generalization below)		

The key is to extend the assessment beyond the demonstration of the targeted knowledge or skill, to include an assessment of conceptual understanding about the processes students engage in as readers, writers, speakers, listeners, researchers, or presenters.

CONCEPT-BASED CLASSROOM SNAPSHOT 13

Close Listening

As part of a Concept-Based Curriculum unit titled "Issues and Perspectives: The Art of Language" with a dual conceptual lens of *Speaker's Craft/Listener's Craft,* ninth-grade students are exploring the power of oracy and rhetoric to communicate a perspective to a listener. During one mini-inquiry, students investigated the relationship between the concepts of listener, perspective, and rhetorical devices.

Each student identifies a social issue of interest (from the teacher's list of options), and forms a small group with others who chose the same issue. Groups are then asked to locate a podcast or speech someone gave on their chosen topic.

The teacher structures the mini-inquiry so she can guide the students to uncover the generalization, *Listeners analyze rhetorical devices used to advance a line of thinking to better understand why a speaker holds that perspective.*

The teacher poses the question, *What is the relationship between a* *listener's understanding* *of a* *speaker's perspective* *and the speaker's use of* *rhetorical devices?* (C)

Concept-Based Students uncover the important conceptual understandings behind complex and abstract skills.

To begin breaking the question down, students are told they will be listening to their podcast twice.

- Initially, they listen to the podcast as a whole and come to consensus as to what they think the speaker's perspective is on the issue.
- While listening a second time, they pay careful attention to the rhetorical devices the speaker used to communicate this perspective. Students then list these devices on paper.
- The group discusses how the rhetoric impacted their understanding of the speaker's perspective.
- Next, the class considers the question, "Why is it important to recognize rhetorical devices and to understand how they can advance a speaker's perspective?" (C)

Finally, students individually complete the activity below.

A Cure for the Most Boring Speech!

1. Research one of the most boring speeches you have heard (from TV, YouTube, Internet, history, and so on) or just make one up!
2. Transcribe the first 3 minutes of the speech and make sure you include the citation.
3. Using your understanding of the power of rhetorical devices, rewrite the first 3 minutes of the speech.
4. Our class will be your listeners. You will give the original 3 minutes of the oration followed by your revision of it using rhetorical devices.
5. Share with the class how you selected your rhetorical devices and why.
6. Your classmates will determine whether or not they, as listeners, were able to better understand the perspective presented through your use of rhetorical devices and why.

In an upcoming lesson, students will now be ready to investigate how rhetoric can be used to mask fallacious reasoning or exaggerate evidence!

CONCEPT-BASED CLASSROOM SNAPSHOT 14

Visual Literacy

As part of a curriculum unit titled "Beyond the Surface: Uncovering Messages in Visuals," with a conceptual lens, *Interpretation*, eighth-grade students are investigating the the interplay between a viewer and visual texts as they explore various genres that blend images and few words to convey messages. A portion of the unit is structured as an in-depth genre study designed to develop students' visual literacy skills using graphic novels as the medium. Each student selects her or his own title from a single genre text-set to use as her or his case study. Each week or so the teacher identifies a generalization as a target for instruction, while also building specific comprehension skills important to analyzing and making meaning from visuals.

In one mini-inquiry, students engage in a lesson designed to reach the generalization, *A viewer's interpretation of visual-heavy text requires attention to details, context clues, text features, and layout*. As students read their graphic novel, the teacher asks that they pay careful attention to what they learn about the character through the <u>details</u> in the artwork, *layout* of the text, and visual symbols versus words. *Text features* include *text* <u>boxes</u>, <u>speech bubbles</u>, and <u>words to represent sounds</u>. Students are also asked to notice how changes in the <u>font</u>, such as bold, italics, and colors, communicate differently than the plain font.

Concept-Based Students distinguish between broad (macro) and specific (micro) concepts.

At the end of the week, students come together in groups of three to compare how they interpreted the characters and story line in their individual graphic novel characters. They also share what they did as viewers to uncover this meaning.

At the end of the inquiry, students are asked to rank, in order from macro to micro, the concepts listed below that are critical to a viewer constructing an interpretation of visual-heavy text, and defend their ordering.

Details in artwork

Text features

Speech bubbles

Visual symbols

Text layout

Onomatopoeia (noise or sound words)

Context clues

Text boxes

Text font

CONCEPT-BASED CLASSROOM SNAPSHOT 15

Storytelling

As part of a daily routine, fourth-grade students engage in morning meetings where all students come together in a sharing circle. During this time, students share stories, recount experiences, and discuss pressing issues, which helps them bond together as a learning community. Throughout the year, students work toward mastering several speaking and listening standards from various curriculum units. Rather than isolated skill-based practice, the morning meeting time serves as an authentic way to move students toward mastery of the standards while also reinforcing an understanding of why the skills are relevant and valuable in their lives.

Today, the teacher continues instruction focusing on a target generalization from the Concept-Based Curriculum storytelling unit they are currently working in. *Speakers tell stories and recount experiences in an organized manner, with appropriate facts and relevant descriptive details, to support a listener's understanding and enjoyment.*

Concept-Based Students mirror the types of authentic literacy processes they will most likely continue to use in their future.

To guide students to speaker and listener generalizations, the teacher uses the morning meeting as another teaching opportunity. He wants to give students time to reflect on the processes of speaking and listening. Sometimes students do this through written reflections, while other times it is through a structured partner discussion. The guiding questions (see below) from the current storytelling unit help path students' thinking from a specific example to thinking about how the example represents the larger process concept—*effective communication*. The teacher provides sentence stems relevant to the generalization to support students who need a "running start" to clearly articulate complex ideas.

Sentence Stem Examples

- I was able to follow the order of the events because the speaker . . .
- The details that helped me understand the speaker's story include . . .
- I understand the story that the speaker is telling because . . .
- I got confused when . . .
- When I am sharing a story, I help people understand by . . .
- The facts (or details) I enjoyed the most . . .
- I show I am listening by . . .
- Sometimes I stop listening when . . .

Ongoing Inquiry Into Speaking, Listening, and Effective Communication
Target Generalization: *Speakers tell stories and recount experiences in an organized manner with appropriate facts and relevant descriptive details to support a listener's understanding and enjoyment.*
Sample Guiding Questions 1. When someone tells a story to recount an experience, what helps you understand what they are saying? (F) 2. When you are telling a story, what do you do to help other students understand and enjoy your story? (F) 3. Think about your favorite story from the week. How did you feel when you were listening? What did the speaker do to help you feel this way? (F) 4. Why do people share stories? (C) 5. How do relevant facts and descriptive details help speakers tell stories so listeners can understand and enjoy them? (C) 6. Why are effective speaking skills important? (C) 7. Can there be too many facts and details in a story? Explain. (D)

The morning meetings are the means to reinforce students' learning about the process of being effective speakers and listeners in a context beyond the storytelling unit work.

CONCEPT-BASED CLASSROOM SNAPSHOT 16

I Can Statements

In a mini-unit titled "Painting Pictures With Words," with a conceptual lens of *Imagery*, fifth-graders have been investigating how authors create connections for readers through the words they choose and how they use them. Instruction has been moving students closer to constructing one of the unit generalizations, *Writers use precise language, sensory details, and varied sentence structures to help create mental images for their readers.*

The teacher wants to provoke students' synergistic thinking at the beginning of his next class. He used to open a lesson by posting objectives as *I Can Statements*. For example, "I can use a variety of sentence structures and types in my writing." Yes, students will know what is expected in the lesson, but as a new Concept-Based teacher, he now posts learning targets as questions to be answered by the end of the lesson, which engages students' conceptual minds and supports their synergistic thinking.

"Today, we are going to explore the question, *Why do writers use different sentence structures and types when they craft a text?"* (C) (Note that the instructional target clarity is not lost.) He then structures a learning experience that asks student partners, (with each partnership receiving an excerpt of a different piece of enlarged text) to first cut the text into sentences. Next, students are asked to scrutinize the sentence structures and types, and to use an open sort to place the sentence strips under concept categories, which they label on notecards (for example, Simple, Compound, Complex, Declarative, Interrogative, Exclamatory). The teacher monitors the work and provides support where needed.

Concept-Based Students move from "doing" to "knowing and understanding" why we do what we do as readers, writers, speakers, and listeners.

Next, as a class, they discuss their findings. *Was only one sentence structure used in their text excerpt?* (F) *Was there only one type of sentence in their text excerpt?* (F) *How many variations did they find?* (F) *And, what was the effectiveness of having different sentence structures and types within a text?* (C)

Students are now ready to move on to explore the how and why behind a writer's sentence structures and types. The teacher asks, *"I'm wondering, how do writers create sentence variety in a text?"* (C) Students go back to comparing the different variations of sentences from their text excerpts as they consider the *how*. Next, the teacher facilitates a writing minilesson where he models techniques to combine, expand, or reduce sentences before he releases the students to work on their independent writing. Students conclude that using different structures and types of sentences makes writing more interesting and often clearer for readers.

During the remainder of the writer's workshop block, the teacher holds writing conferences where he continues to guide students incrementally toward the generalization by asking students to reflect on the impact their sentences will have on their readers' mental images.

Students were expected to do the work and thinking. The result is that their learning will be more meaningful and memorable. The skill in the "I Can Statement" was not lost; it is just taught in a more conceptual and thought-provoking way. Subsequent lessons will focus on investigating remaining concepts within the generalization and their relationships, before students are expected to synthesize the information and articulate their understanding of how writers help create mental images for readers.

Summary

As literacy teachers, often we assume that the mastery of a complex skill, such as elementary students finding the main idea of texts, equates to the ability to automatically transfer that skill to new situations, when in fact it does not. In *Visible Learning for Literacy,* authors Fisher, Frey, and Hattie (2016) explain that . . .

> With appropriate instruction about how to relate and extend ideas, surface learning becomes deep understanding. Deep understanding is important if students are going to set their own expectations and monitor their own achievement. But schooling should not stop there. Learning demands that students be able to apply and transfer their knowledge, skills, and strategies to new tasks and new situations. That transfer is so difficult to attain is one of our closely kept secrets—so often we pronounce that students can transfer, but the process of teaching them this still is too often not discussed. (pp. 18–19) . . . The ultimate goal, and one that is hard to realize, is transfer.

Teaching for transfer is the aspect of literacy teaching and learning that gets us excited! Knowing that how we develop knowledge, skills, and conceptual understanding *simultaneously* in our literacy classrooms makes a difference. Our hope is that the various classroom Snapshots help to demystify the process of teaching for conceptual understanding and transfer, and leave you feeling empowered to begin experimenting in your own classroom.

In the resource section, we will also show you a few more ways to support inductive inquiry in a Concept-Based literacy classroom that include examples of 3D graphic organizers.

Extending Thought

How comfortable do you feel about making a shift in your instructional practices so that students' learning experiences move beyond knowledge and skills? If you need a jump start, consider the following tips as additional layers to add to familiar instructional techniques and classroom practices.

1. Use concepts to create an interplay between the factual and conceptual levels. This ignites *synergistic thinking.*
2. Provide multiple text options to allow students to uncover conceptual patterns, and to promote student choice. This cultivates *critical thinking.*
3. Create opportunities for students to reflect on the process they engaged in during the learning experience. Can students explain why they do what they do as readers, writers, speakers, listeners, and viewers? This promotes *reflective thinking.*

Although the tips appear to be simple shifts, don't underestimate their power. When used together, they can add a whole new dimension to your classroom. As you can see, thinking students require thinking teachers. What is one small shift in your practice that you can make today?

CHAPTER 5

Frequently Asked Questions

FIGURE 5.1

Do you feel the way we do? The more we learn, the more questions we seem to have. We see this as a positive way to continuously deepen our understanding. Below we address some common questions we hear from our Concept-Based literacy audiences. If you have others, don't hesitate to send them to us. We look forward to you joining us on our journey to transform literacy learning!

1. *How does Concept-Based Curriculum "fit in" with some of the popular literacy resources on the market?*

The Daily 5, Reading Essentials, and the Workshop Model provide an instructional framework, or delivery system, for a Concept-Based Curriculum. CBCI fits naturally with these and many other resources, which represent proven ways to manage instructional time and to support literacy learning. The materials in these resources represent high-quality literacy practices, but conceptual understanding is not their focus. Concept-Based Curriculum adds the third dimension (conceptual understanding) as a learning target. CBCI addresses what students will *Know, Understand,* and be able to *Do* as a result of their learning. The teacher decides which instructional approaches will most effectively deliver the curriculum and help students meet *each* of the three types of learning targets.

2. *Why such a comprehensive Concept-Based lesson plan?*

Cognitive research supports designing conceptual curriculum and instruction to align teaching with the way people learn. However, this research is still unfamiliar to many teachers. Concept-Based lesson planning takes time—initially a lot of time—because we are moving away from how we, for the most part, were trained as educators and how we learned in school. Writing a Concept-Based lesson plan requires thinking: Thinking about the conceptual, transferable ideas essential to the subject area, about how to design learning experiences that are intellectually and emotionally engaging, and about how to move each of our students forward. The Concept-Based lesson planner is structured to help keep you on the right track as you design instruction. Because robust and rigorous generalizations take students time to uncover and construct, one lesson plan may span across 3–5 classes or days with continuous adjusting based on how the students are progressing. From our own experiences and from the testimonies of teachers we have worked with, we find the time put into lesson planning is well worth the results we see in students. A comprehensive lesson plan is one way to maximize teaching efficiency in the long run.

3. *How does Concept-Based literacy meet the needs of diverse learners? (English Language Learners, Special Education students, students of trauma, and so on)? Will struggling students get enough literacy support in an inquiry-based classroom?*

This is a question that we hear frequently. All students are capable of engaging in meaningful contextualized learning, but it does take well-thought-out, intentional support and guidance. Chapter 3 discussed the place for explicit instruction in conjunction with inquiry to guide students to a conceptual understanding.

Concept-Based Curriculum works to make learning whole and coherent by first anchoring learning in authentic contexts and then setting a purpose for students' inquiry work. Dissecting and analyzing parts, or bits of learning, won't make sense or seem relevant to learners unless there is an understanding of the relationship between the parts to a greater "whole." It is a natural tendency for teachers to want to simplify complex processes, break learning into small, easy-to-manage chunks, and ultimately do the thinking for students, especially for those who appear to be struggling. The problem with this approach is that on any given day, these students rarely, if ever, have the opportunity to construct meaning on their own.

In *Culturally Responsive Teaching and the Brain* (2015, pp. 14–15), Zaretta Hammond explains that:

> As educators, we have to recognize that we help maintain the achievement gap when we don't teach advance cognitive skills to students we label as "disadvantaged" because of their language, gender, race or socioeconomic status.
>
> Based on these labels, we usually do the following (Means & Knapp, 1991):
>
> - Underestimate what disadvantaged students are intellectually capable of doing.
> - As a result, we postpone more challenging and interesting work until we believe they have mastered "the basics."
> - By focusing only on low-level basics, we deprive students of a meaningful or motivating context for learning and practicing higher order thinking processes.

When literacy is taught as series of isolated skills in decontextualized learning experiences, students are robbed of experiencing what it means to be a capable reader, writer, speaker, and listener. Concept-Based Literacy teachers do not assume students need to master the basics before engaging in inquiry. In fact, quite the opposite is true. When teachers implement the curriculum through authentic, accessible experiences that mirror the types of knowledge and processes students will most likely continue to use in their future, understanding is advanced. Finally, when the curriculum is designed to stimulate thought, reflection, and ownership of learning, students are more motivated to learn, which makes the learning experience far more memorable (Lanning, 2013).

Inductive inquiry does not equate to unsupported or unstructured learning experiences or learning that is not grounded in literacy standards. Planning ways to differentiate learning and to use techniques designed to support diverse learners are both essential components of Concept-Based literacy classrooms. The content, process, product, and the learning environment can be differentiated, but not the conceptual understanding (generalization). Remember, within the framework of a Concept-Based lesson, teachers select classroom practices to best match the needs of the unique students in their classrooms.

This includes practices common to many classrooms, such as:

- Texts at appropriate reading levels
- Graphic organizers to scaffold thinking
- Alternate ways to interpret and communicate key concepts, such as through images
- Strategic student grouping
- Additional instruction through small group work—See Balancing Inductive Inquiry and Explicit Instruction in Chapter 3
- Varying amounts of teacher guidance
- Productive feedback
- Sentence stems
- Strategies for second language acquisition
- A range of authentic assessments and options to communicate learning
- Opportunities for student choice
- Focus on personal meaning making and relevance
- Technological tools to increase access

4. *How does Concept-Based Literacy fit with interventions, or support services?*

The support service model varies from district to district. We've personally experienced success when the Concept-Based Curriculum is taught in conjunction with "Push-In" services or a co-teaching model. In a Push-In model, support specialists join the general education classroom to provide services while students are engaged in the core curriculum. The Push-In model works well with Concept-Based Literacy because it allows all students to access a quality core curriculum while also receiving the necessary support services. This system is very beneficial to students but does require some extra collaboration between the general education teacher and the teacher specialists.

Here's an example of what this collaboration could look like:

> Special Education and Consultant Teacher Connie Walser, from Burlington-Edison School District, Burlington, WA, supports sixth- to eighth-grade students in a Push-In model. To ensure students are making continuous progress, she schedules weekly

meetings with the general education teachers to co-plan lessons for the upcoming week. Connie asks the teachers to explain their learning goals for the week, including conceptual understanding. Then she considers this through the lens of the students she serves with Individual Education Plans. She often includes the school's Speech and Language Pathologist and the English Language Learner teacher to engage in the collaboration. Her focus is on helping ensure equitable access to the quality core curriculum and to ensure that needed supports are in place during the learning experiences.

Connie reflects on the power of the Push-in model and co-planning:

> Inquiry has closed the door to the "resource room" model and opened the door to the thinking classroom. No longer are students isolated because their lagging skills prevent them from learning with their peers. Instead, teachers and other service providers are collaboratively bringing their expertise to the table to plan for learning experiences that are accessible to all students. There is magic in co-planning inquiry experiences with 2, 3, or 4 brains in the mix. Together, colleagues with varying areas of expertise can help create bridges for students who communicate, process information, read, and write differently than their peers. Students with less proficient literacy skills can thrive in an inquiry classroom where questioning, curiosity, and thinking are the necessary tools. ALL kids can do that! Discovering knowledge can take many routes, and technology, more and more, is providing alternate paths to information. Careful co-planning is the key. It takes time to find your rhythm and role with your colleagues. Time, however, is a small price. Inquiry classrooms create space for students to build skills that are important for life; confidence, perseverance, communication, problem-solving savvy, and the ability to value and build on the thinking of others. While more difficult to measure, these learning and thinking behaviors are the backbone of successful, meaningful community members. By creating learning experiences where all students can thrive, we honor our differences and embrace our collective fabulousness.

If a Push-In model is not an option in your setting, or if your system operates with a "Core + More" model, consider how you can include concepts from the Concept-Based Curriculum Unit with the skill development occurring in the Pull-Out services. Also, we have seen many schools successfully use the Pull-Out model to provide additional, explicit skill instruction, while *making sure* students are back in the classroom for the learning experiences directly tied to the Concept-Based lesson. Regardless of the support service model in your school, we advocate an approach that maintains contextualized literacy learning for all students as a top priority.

5. *Does Concept-Based Literacy provide enough challenge for Gifted or Highly Capable students?*

Yes! Concept-Based Curriculum and Instruction easily extends beyond a core curriculum even though Concept-Based is for ALL learners. In a conceptual curriculum, there is no limit to the extent students can deepen their learning, more independently expand their inquiries, or increase the magnitude of connected concepts. The bottom line is, the third dimension of CBCI provides opportunities to naturally enhance learning expectations.

Let's think about this fifth-grade example in Table 5.1:

In a two-dimensional classroom, teachers might extend learning by providing a more complex text for gifted students to read, or they might layer on more questions at the end of the

TABLE 5.1 TWO-DIMENSIONAL LITERACY COMPARED TO THREE-DIMENSIONAL LITERACY EXPERIENCE

CCSS.ELA-LITERACY.RL.5.2	
Determine a theme of a story, drama, or poem from details in the text, including how characters in a story or drama respond to challenges or how the speaker in a poem reflects upon a topic; summarize the text.	
Two-Dimensional Literacy Experience	Three-Dimensional Literacy Experience
All students read a short story from the basal reader and answer five questions designed to assess students' comprehension of the text. Two questions are targeted to specific details in the story: one question is about the theme, one question is about how a character responds to a challenge, and for the final question students are asked to summarize the story.	Students are exploring the relationship between *theme and characters' response to challenges.* As one step in determining the theme of a story, the teacher wants students to uncover the generalization of *Authors create dynamic characters that grow and change in response to events of a plot.* Students form into small groups, with each group reading a different story. Students discuss how the protagonist responds to challenges and reflect on what happens to the character as a result of this challenge. Groups share out as a class so that they can notice patterns across several texts. Students realize that all of their characters experienced growth and changed as a result of the events of the plot. Many students quickly connect this to their own lives and to how they've grown as a response to personal challenges. *While we could go on to describe more of the learning progression, we will pause here.*

story, or they may even add an "enrichment" activity to be completed while other students are finishing their work. At first glance this appears to provide a more rigorous learning experience, but did the student really gain any greater depth of understanding? Now contrast this with the three-dimensional example in the scenario above. There is no ceiling or limit to how far a student could take the learning experience. Imagine all of the different directions they could go! Notice how the three-dimensional example naturally went beyond the skill addressed in the standard to also develop conceptual understanding, and it allowed students to find personal relevance that extends beyond the typical learner.

6. *Isn't mastering the skills articulated in the standards enough?*

Concept-Based teachers often answer questions from students with questions, so let's first consider this through a couple of questions.

- Does mastering a standard ensure that students understand *why* they do what they do as readers, writers, speakers, and listeners?
- How can you be sure that mastering a standard leads to the transfer of learning to new and inevitably more complex situations?
- Does mastering a standard equate to deeply understanding the role of literacy in our daily lives and in our global society?

Mastering the standards is a crucial step in the learning process, but it is not the end goal in and of itself. "This takes us to the point that an ample number of the suggested learning experiences must be designed so that students truly demonstrate and are able to articulate their understanding. Students may be required to complete work examples (write an essay, story, diagram, play, etc.), but if they are not pushed beyond to reflect on the process, integrate knowledge, explain the choices made, and express the conceptual idea [understanding] represented by the product, the learning experience falls short of our curriculum goal" (Lanning, 2013, p. 97). We need to cultivate readers, writers, speakers, and listeners who are confident transacting with *any* type of text that they will encounter in the future, and who have the skill set needed to communicate their own ideas through platforms that we haven't even dreamt yet. Consider the recent rise of podcasts, or of infographics! Twenty years ago, we were not training children to master the skills needed to decipher a complex infographic. We can't predict what our students are going to encounter in the next twenty years, so it is essential that we help students grow a deep-rooted sense of what it means to be a literate member of a global community, in addition to demonstrating competency in the skills articulated in our current standards.

7. *How do you ensure vertical alignment? Specifically, how do you ensure that the generalizations are progressively more complex?*

Without a curriculum master plan, teachers teach "stuff" and students learn, but it may not be the right "stuff" or have relevance to what lies ahead. Ensuring that curriculum is vertically aligned allows students the opportunity to discover the intricacies of a discipline one well-planned year at a time. In English language arts, concepts such as character remain constant across the grades, but a student's understanding of the intricacies of the concept must become more specific with age and maturity. The Common Core State Standards spiral, which helps skills and concepts to be unpacked to a greater depth each year.

Let's think again about the macroconcept of character. In kindergarten, understanding the concept of "character" is a big idea and an important concept in understanding text. By the secondary grade levels, students demonstrate a greater depth of understanding as they discuss and analyze the microconcepts, "static characters," "protagonists." "antagonists," "dynamic characters," "round characters," and the like. In order to increase depth of understanding through the grade levels, the macroconcepts need to be emptied out to the more specific microconcepts that lie underneath. The more micro (specific) the concept is, the more expertise it takes to understand it. In other words, the progression of curriculum units will build depth of understanding as concepts become more exact. Think about this: what separates a novice from an expert in a discipline? It's the understanding of more microconcepts that takes greater expertise.

Let's look at what this might look like across the fourth- to tenth-grade span. In Table 5.2 below, notice how the macroconcept *character* remains constant. For each grade level, microconcepts are drawn out to add more specificity at each grade level. We move from microconcepts such as *character traits* in fourth grade, to *dynamic* and *static characters* in seventh grade, to *intrinsic versus extrinsic motivations* by tenth grade. As students move through the grades, they are expected to uncover an increasingly sophisticated understanding of the concept of *character.*

TABLE 5.2 MACROCONCEPTS TO MORE MICROCONCEPTS

	Fourth Grade	Seventh Grade	Tenth Grade
Macroconcept Microconcepts	*Character* *character traits*	*Character* *dynamic character, static character*	*Character* *complex character, intrinsic vs. extrinsic motivation, internal vs. external conflicts, character relationships*
Generalization	Readers discover character traits through a character's thoughts, actions, dialogue, and relationships.	Authors use elements of a story and static characters to imply changes in a dynamic character.	Authors create complex characters with varied and conflicting motivations, internal and external conflicts, and relationships with other characters to advance the plot and develop the theme of a story.

Through intentionally designed progressions, teachers can be sure that each year the students will gain a deeper, more precise understanding of the concepts important to the discipline. The generalizations increase in complexity grade-to-grade through the intentional inclusion of microconcepts, as shown above. A well-thought-out, vertically aligned, Concept-Based Curriculum provides teachers with a clear master plan designed to guide students to continuous development of disciplinary expertise.

8. *What is the role of assessment in a Concept-Based classroom?*

In Concept-Based classrooms, we assess students in three areas: (1) Content knowledge, (2) Understanding, and (3) Process.

Through authentic formative and summative assessments, we consider:

- How well are students mastering the academic standards (Processes and Skills)?
- How deep is students' understanding of the key concepts and generalizations under study?
- Are students seeing the relevance between what they are learning and their lives outside of school?

Every learning experience has the potential to provide the teacher with valuable information about students' progress toward learning goals. Observation of student dialogue, exit tickets, answers written on individual whiteboards, formal writing tasks, reading conferences, sticky note reflections—all serve as assessments for gaining information about student learning and for using that data to inform future instruction.

While Concept-Based teachers continually assess students' progress toward the academic standards, they also gather data through a variety of methods to monitor students' developing conceptual understanding. This is a key difference from other types of curriculum design frameworks. Often teachers *assume* that students understand concepts and generalizations important to the discipline, but Concept-Based teachers actually assess students to *ensure* that conceptual understanding and transfer have been reached.

For example, imagine that a group of eighth-grade students are exploring the relationship between sensory language and the conveyance of experiences and events while reading and writing personal narratives. From a holistic perspective, beyond a narrative writing score on the assessment rubric, look at the information that can be gained when assessing conceptual understanding through multiple types of data points:

- Teacher's observation of the student's participation in a small-group discussion analyzing a mentor text
- Teacher's notes taken during a writing conference discussing the student's use of sensory language in their draft of a personal narrative
- Observational data of student's dialogue during a peer writing conference
- Teacher's notes taken during a reading conference discussing the author's use of sensory language and their personal connections with their independent reading novels
- Student's sticky-note reflection after a concept sort
- Student responses to a perception survey assessing relevance of the learning to the student's life outside of school
- Student personal narrative sharing a meaningful life experience

- Students' craft reports accompanying their final piece of writing, which explains the choices in writing techniques used and why
- Students' articulation of a target process generalization

All of these examples give rich insight into a student's growing conceptual understanding, in conjunction with the skill-based writing score traditionally assigned. Additionally, assessing students through authentic contexts is key to ensuring student's see how their learning transfers beyond the particular lesson. Resource C-1 further explains the role of Student Self-Reflection and Self-Assessment in a Concept-Based Literacy classroom. Resource C-2 outlines how teachers can use Craft Reports as assessments of conceptual understanding.

9. *How do students react to Concept-Based Instruction?*

Of course, in the end, the hard work that teachers do in classrooms each day is about the impact on students. So, we give the final word to one student who experienced the shift to a Concept-Based literacy classroom.

My eighth-grade English Language Arts experience was amazing! My learning was very different from my previous, and even current Language Arts courses. My classmates and I were encouraged to ask questions and inquire. Inquiring really helped me understand text deeper, and I felt much more engaged. I have been able to apply my learning in other learning situations now in high school. I felt very involved in class when we learned through Concept-Based teaching. When we worked on our Night projects I really felt like I understood the big ideas and I had a lot of fun working on it. I was really engaged with everything and it really made me want to put the effort in. I feel like my understanding of that learning has helped me.

In earlier English classes, we collaborated only a little, or not at all. We mainly focused on writing essays and using correct conventions. In this ELA class, we researched and wrote essays while collaborating with our classmates. Our collaboration included Socratic Seminars, and Fish Bowls. Our main goal was to go deeper into the text and really understand what it was about conceptually. Overall my middle school Language Arts class was really influential to me as a reader and writer. I am now able to transfer my learning to similar content. As I reflect on everything that we learned I'm grateful for my experience with Concept-Based learning. I have realized how great my learning really was. Thank you, Mrs. Brown!

—Makenzie

Resources

Resource A: Model CBCI Curriculum Units

A-1 Overview of Model Units

Learning From Model Unit Plans

In Chapter 3, we analyzed and reflected on Model Lesson plans as a way to share more about Concept-Based lesson planning. The model units in this resource are also used as a tool to further deepen your understanding.

All five model units provide examples of the essential components of Concept-Based Curriculum units:

- Unit Title
- Conceptual Lens
- Unit Overview
- Unit Web
- Generalizations
- Guiding Questions
- Critical Content and Key Skills
- Learning Experiences
- Culminating Assessment
- Scoring Guide

Model Unit 1 shows the Grade 10 Concept-Based Curriculum unit that was referenced throughout the process of writing the literacy lesson plan showcased in Chapter 2. This is an example of a fully completed Concept-Based Curriculum literacy unit.

Model Units 2–5 are unique in that each provides you with all the elements of a Concept-Based unit completed except for the Learning Experiences and some of the scoring guides. These "almost complete" Model Units 2–4 serve as teaching tools for you to learn about writing lessons from a Concept-Based literacy curriculum unit for your students. You will notice that the Learning Experience pages in Units 2–5 build on each other and then ask new questions to take your thinking one step further.

The scoring guides for Model Units 3–5 are also structured to build on each other and nudge your thinking with new questions. Each model unit adds a new variation of scoring guides for you to consider. This will help you see the wide range of possibilities so that you can best meet the needs of the learners in your school setting.

The model units are designed to not only serve as examples but to also build your expertise as a CBCI teacher. Together the model units provide a wide a wealth of information to deepen your understanding and sharpen your skills.

Resource A-2 ***Model Unit 1***

Grade 10

Title: The Art of Argumentation

Resource A-3 ***Model Unit 2***

Grade 8

Title: Dystopian Societies: Could This Really Be Our Future?

Resource A-4 ***Model Unit 3***

Grade 7

Title: Every Voice Counts: The Struggle for Equity

Resource A-5 ***Model Unit 4***

Grade 9

Title: Oh the Choice Authors Face!

Resource A-6 ***Model Unit 5***

Grade 5

Title: Personal Narratives: Here's My Story

Resource A-2 Grade 10 *The Art of Argumentation*

Grade Level: 10

Unit Number: 4

Unit Title: *The Art of Argumentation*

Conceptual *Lens*: *Argumentation*

Unit Length: Approximately 6–7 weeks

Unit Overview:

Think of the last time you were in an argument or listened to an argument. Describe what was happening. Was the point of the argument effectively communicated? Was the argument based more on personal opinion and emotions or was support for the claim logically structured, clearly researched (from both sides), and substantiated with factual evidence? Argumentation doesn't need to be viewed as something negative. An argument needn't dissolve into a contest of whose voice is the loudest! Crafting an effective argument is an art. In a world that blasts you with information and claims each day, it is important to know what to think, why we think what we do, and how to advance an argument effectively. That's what this unit is about. Are you ready to argue?

Technology Integration:

- Multimedia
- Internet

Standards or national curricula addressed in this unit:

CCSS.ELA-LITERACY.RI9-10.1
CCSS.ELA-LITERACY.R19-10.2
CCSS.ELA-LITERACY.RI9-10.3
CCSS.ELA-LITERACY.RI.9-10.5
CCSS.ELA-LITERACY.RI.9-10.6
CCSS.ELA-LITERACY.RI.9-10.8
CCSS.ELA-LITERACY.W.9-10.1a
CCSS.ELA-LITERACY.W.9-10.1b
CCSS.ELA-LITERACY.W.9-10.1c
CCSS.ELA-LITERACY.W.9-10.1d
CCSS.ELA-LITERACY.SL9-10.1a
CCSS.ELA-LITERACY.SL9-10.1c
CCSS.ELA-LITERACY.SL9-10.3

Unit Title: *The Art of Argumentation*
Grade Level: 10

Conceptual Lens: Argumentation

Strand 1: Understanding Text

- Components of an argument
- Critical reading strategies
- Inference
- Close reading
- Author's purpose
- Claim
- Reasons
- Evidence
- Rhetoric

Strand 2: Responding to Text

- Discussion of reasons and types of support/evidence
- Connections
- Group member responsibilities
- Relevant questions
- Reflection
- Perspective

Unit Title:

The Art of Argumentation

Strand 3: Critiquing Text

- Criteria of an effective argument
- Trustworthiness
- Quality and credibility of sources
- Relevance
- Validity
- Sound vs. fallacious reasoning
- Counterclaim

Strand 4: Producing Text

- Attributes of target audience
- Argumentative techniques
- Counterarguments
- Elaboration
- Concise claim
- Text cohesion

Unit Title: *The Art of Argumentation* **Conceptual Lens:** Argumentation
Grade Level: 10

Generalizations	Guiding Questions: F=Factual; C=Conceptual; D=Debatable
1. The effective organization of the components of an argument advance an author's claim.	1a. What are the components of an argument? (F) 1b. What types of evidence can be used to support the reasons offered in an argument? (specific examples, statistics, data, testimonies, counterclaims, etc.) (F) 1c. What claim is the author (or speaker) of ___ making?(F) 1d. Why is a powerful claim statement important? (C) 1e. How did the author organize the argument presented in the text? (F) 1f. How did the author's organization of the argument impact your understanding of the claim? (F) 1g. How does the organization of the components of an argument impact an author's claim? (C)
2. People who read critically (question, challenge, verify information, and so on) avoid being misinformed.	2a. What is critical reading? (F) 2b. What are some of the consequences of being misinformed? (F) 2c. What strategies do readers use to evaluate an argument? (F) 2d. Why is it important to uncover fallacious reasoning or weak evidence in an argument? (C) 2e. How do critical literacy skills empower people? (C) 2f. How much responsibility lies with a reader in avoiding "fake news"? (D)
3. Effective group member responsibilities foster a deeper understanding for everyone.	3a. What are important group member responsibilities? (F) 3b. How can considering the insights, reactions, and different perspectives of others help deepen understanding for everyone? (C) 3c. Why is the preparedness of each group member critical to the effectivness of the entire group ? (C)
4. Analyzing the quality and credibility of sources cited in text helps determine whether or not a claim is trustworthy.	4a. Who published your text? Who is the author? (F) 4b. Is the claim in your text supported by valid evidence? (F) 4c. Why are primary sources more credible than secondary sources? (C) 4d. Why is currency an important consideration (when the source was published)? (C) 4e. How does an author's reliability strengthen his/her credibility? (C)
5. Knowledge of an audience enables writers to develop a more credible and compelling argument.	5a. What must writers consider about an audience when selecting support for a claim? (F) 5b. How do counterclaims contribute to an argument? (C) 5c. How does a writer learn the common characteristics of a target audience? (C)

Critical Content and Key Skills

Critical Content by Strands	Key Skills
Students will know . . .	**Students will be able to . . .**
Strand 1: Understanding Text • Criteria of strong evidence supporting a claim • Central idea vs. specific details • The components of an argument • Types of evidence	CCSS.ELA-LITERACY.RI9-10.1: Cite strong and thorough textual evidence to support analysis of what the text says explicitly as well as inferences drawn from texts. CCSS.ELA-LITERACY.R19-10.2: Determine a central idea of a text and analyze its development over course of the text, including how it emerges and is shaped and refined by specific details.
Strand 2: Responding to Text • Relevant questions • Group member responsibilities • Sentence stems to propel conversations (clarify, verify, challenge ideas)	CCSS.ELA-LITERACY.SL9-10.1C: Propel conversations by posing and responding to questions that relate the current discussion to broader themes or larger ideas; actively incorporate others into the discussion; and clarify, verify, or challenge ideas and conclusions. CCSS.ELA-LITERACY.SL.9-10.1a: Come to discussions prepared, having rad and researched material under study; explicitly draw on that preparation by referring to evidence from texts and other research on the topic or issue to stimulate a thoughtful, well-reasoned exchange of ideas.
Strand 3: Critiquing Text • Techniques used to analyze and evaluate an argument • Fallacious reasoning; exaggerated/distorted evidence • Effective organization of the components of an argument • Valid evidence/reasoning • Rhetorical language	CCSS ELA-SL.9-10.3: Evaluate a speaker's point of view, reasoning, and use of evidence and rhetoric, identifying any fallacious reasoning or exaggerated or distorted evidence. CCSS.ELA-LITERACY.RI.9-10.8: Delineate and evaluate the argument and specific claims in a text, assessing whether the reasoning is valid and the evidence is relevant and sufficient; identify false statements and fallacious reasoning.
Strand 4: Producing Text • Meaning of claims, counter claims • Attributes of target audience • Various argumentative techniques • Different types of mediums, visuals and multimedia • Traits of effective analogies	CCSS.ELA-LITERACY.RI.9-10.5: Analyze in detail how an author's ideas or claims are developed and refined by particular sentences, paragraphs, or larger portions of text (e.g., a section of a chapter). CCSS.ELA-LITERACY.W.9-10.1a: Introduce precise claim(s), distinguish the claim(s) from alternate or opposing claims, and create an organization that establishes clear relationships among claim(s), counterclaims, reasons. CCSS.ELA-LITERACY.W.9-10.1b: Develop claim(s) fairly, supplying evidence for each while pointing out the strengths and limitations of both in a manner that anticipates the audience's knowledge level and concerns. CCSS.ELA-LITERACY.W.9-10.c: Use words, phrases, and clauses to link the major section of the text, create cohesion, and clarify the relationship between claims and reasons, between reasons and evidence, and between claims and counterclaims. CCSS-ELA. W.11-12.2.D: Use precise language, domain-specific vocabulary, and techniques such as metaphor, simile, and analogy to manage the complexity of the topic.

Unit Title: *Art of Argumentation*
Grade Level: 10

Suggested Time Line	Suggested Learning Experiences (Note: G#=Target Generalization GQ=Guiding Questions)	Assessments	Differentiation	Resources
Weeks 1–2	Introduction: Pose an engaging conceptual opening question about argumentation. Capture student responses on a class T-Chart with headings: *Audience, Impact.* Update throughout unit.			
	Inquiry 1: Exploring Organization and Impact *[NOTE: See completed lesson plan in Figure 2.6]* Introduce components of an argument, discuss the relationship of the components, and define each. • Design an inductive activity using different models of argumentative texts so that students can discover how arguments are organized • Using new text examples and GQ #1a–1g, guide students in evaluating the effectiveness of Argument • Students synthesize information from their small-group chart and individually create an analogy that expresses the relationship among organization of the components of an argument and the impact of the author's claim. (G#1)	Observation and quality of student responses Group observation and conferencing Review small-group chart Individual Analogy of G#1	Small-group configurations	Artifact Box: Include 5–7 excerpts from different text sources that exemplify the essential components of effective arguments (articles, cartoons, ads, and so forth)
Week 3	**Inquiry 2: Exploring Claims and Credibility** • Ask student groups to return to the texts used in Inquiry #1. • Using GQ#4a–e, have groups investigate the quality and credibility of the sources cited in each of the texts in their artifact file. • At the end of their investigation, each group completes the sentence, "We understand that . . ."	Group articulation of G#4	Text examples at different readability levels and different types	
	Inquiry 3: Exploring Critical Reading and Misinformation • Model (think-aloud) critical reading of an argumentative article presenting a claim about a current event topic. • Individually, students engage in close reading of a second argumentative article presenting the opposing side of the issue in the first article. • Using Fishbowl technique, have students in the inner circle pose questions and discuss the contents of both articles and evaluate the claim, reasoning, evidence, and counterclaim. Students in inner circle discuss, share; students in outer circle listen, observe, and take notes. • Students switch places, and the new inner circle holds a discussion while the outer circle observes. • After the discussion, have students form triads to reflect on the process of reading texts critically. Pose GQ #2b–2e.	Student responses Teacher observation Student reflection Observation and quality of student responses	Small-group configurations Teacher support or extension as needed Sentence stems to propel conversations (clarify, verify, challenge ideas)	Text for Think-Aloud

(Continued)

(Continued)

Weeks 4–5	**Inquiry 4: Exploring Collaboration and Understanding Text** Ask whole class to review group member responsibilities and rationale for each. • Use guiding questions for G#3 to draw students' thinking toward G#3. • Ask students to use writing journals to write a reflection of the effectiveness of their discussion during their inquiry work. • Guide students thinking to G#3.	Group observation and conferencing	Small-group configurations	
Weeks 6–7	**Week of Hot Topics: Question, Challenge, and Verify** • Small groups identify a Hot Topic in the news and conducts research to locate two articles (presenting each side of the issue). Students apply their understanding of G#1, G#2, G#3, and G#4 as they evaluate potential articles. • Groups take turns leading the class through a process of close reading of their articles. This is a time for students to engage critical thinking and academic discourse skills. • Students individually reflect on GQ# 2e and take a stance on GQ# 2f. (G#2) **Assign the Culminating Unit Assessment**	Observation and quality of student responses Collective class articulation of G#2 Scoring guide	Support written texts with visuals, videos, or additional scaffolding based on student need Sentence stems to propel conversations	Access to the internet for research

Culminating Unit Assessment

Unit Title: *The Art of Argumentation* **Conceptual Lens:** Argumentation
Grade Level: 10

What (the unit focus): Students will investigate the art of crafting an argument,

Why (the generalization or generalizations): in order to understand that . . .

Knowledge of an audience enables writers to develop a more credible and compelling argument.

How (the engaging scenario for students): Throughout this unit, we explored the many components of an argument and how authors advance a claim by effectively organizing the components. You also analyzed the quality and credibility of sources in arguments to determine whether or not a claim is trustworthy.

Your assignment is to now apply what you learned these past weeks and craft an argument based on a claim you feel strongly about. You need to first identify the type of audience who will read your argument. (senior citizens, teenagers, community or business leaders, voters, school officials, young mothers, and so forth). The strength of your claim (for example, Quality health care should be a guaranteed right for the elderly.) is dependent on how well you know your audience, anticipate their concerns and address counterclaims (for example, Ensuring quality health care for the elderly is a family responsibility.).

Step 1: Choose your audience (from the class list of community members or volunteer class readers) and write a first draft of the claim you want to make.

Step 2: Research your topic thoroughly—for example, reasons supporting your claim, credible evidence, counterclaims—and anticipate your audience's concerns.

Step 3: Draft your argument to support your claim using valid reasoning and relevant and sufficient evidence. Revise your piece to create cohesion and clarify the relationships between claims(s) and reasons, between reasons and evidence, and between claims and counterclaims. You have 2 weeks to complete your assignment.

Step 4: After crafting your argument, we will share your paper with a member of your target audience who volunteered to be a reader.

Reflection Report: Respond to the following:
1. What did you learn about the characteristics of your target audience?
2. Explain how your knowledge of your target audience enabled you to make a more credible and compelling argument.
3. Think about the process you used to develop your argument based on your learning throughout this unit. How do you expect you might present an argument to someone in your life differently in the future?

Scoring Guide for Letter Grades

Task:

S T A N D A R D

Scoring Criteria	Possible Pts. or %	Self-Assess.	Teacher Assess.
Understanding			
Responses to #1 and #2 in Reflection Report show how knowledge of audience was used to shape the development of an effective argument	40		
Content			
Includes typical attributes of target audience	15		
Accurate information related to claim, counterclaim, reasons, and evidence	15		
Process			
Demonstrates command of organizing the components of an effective argument Uses words, phrases, and clauses to link the major section of the text, create cohesion, and clarify the relationships between claims(s) and reasons, between reasons and evidence, and between claims and counterclaims.	30		
	100	____	____

Scoring Key

A =

B =

C =

I =

Resource A-3 Grade 8 *Dystopian Societies: Could This Really Be Our Future?*

Grade Level: 8
Unit Number: 4

Unit Title: *Dystopian Societies: Could this really be our future?* **Conceptual Lens:** Theme/Critical Analysis

Unit Length: Approximately 8–10 weeks

Unit Overview:

Imagine your perfect society. What does that look like for you? One free of our current struggles and conflicts? What happens if the seemingly perfect society is not so perfect after all? What happens if there is a darker side hiding in hopes of not being discovered? Could such a society ever really come to exist in the future? In this unit, you will critically read a novel featuring a utopian/dystopian society in order to become more critical consumers of the things you encounter in the world around you. You will also build your understanding of the unique traits or elements of this genre of speculative fiction. We will explore various elements of the genre through a series of mini-inquires and collaborative discussions. You will demonstrate your understanding of the author's message and elements of dystopian literature through a critical literary analysis essay.

Technology Integration:

- Word processing
- Digital videos to support learning

Standards or national curricula addressed in this unit:

CCSS.ELA-LITERACY.RL.8.1
CCSS.ELA-LITERACY.RL.8.2
CCSS.ELA-LITERACY.RL.8.3
CCSS.ELA-LITERACY.RL.8.4
CCSS.ELA-LITERACY.RL.8.9
CCSS.ELA-LITERACY.W.8.1
CCSS.ELA-LITERACY.W.8.1A
CCSS.ELA-LITERACY.W.8.1B
CCSS.ELA-LITERACY.W.8.1C
CCSS.ELA-LITERACY.W.8.1E
CCSS.ELA-LITERACY.W.8.3A-E
CCSS.ELA-LITERACY.SL.8.1A
CCSS.ELA-LITERACY.SL.8.1B
CCSS.ELA-LITERACY.SL.8.1C
CCSS.ELA-LITERACY.SL.8.1D
CCSS.ELA-LITERACY.L.8.5

Unit Title: *Dystopian Societies: Could this really be our future?* **Conceptual Lens:** Theme/Critical Analysis
Grade Level: 8

Strand 1: Understanding Text

- Elements of a dystopian society: control, conflict
- Societal values
- Setting or time frame
- Themes: societal control, corruption, oppression, fear, manipulation, survival, hope, rebellion
- Inference
- Deep text analysis
- Allusion

Strand 2: Responding to Text

- Discussion protocols
- Connections
- Personal reflection (What would I do?)
- Influence
- Perspectives; Interpretation
- Probing questions

Unit Title:

Dystopian Societies: Could this really be our future?

Strand 4: Producing Text

- Literary analysis
- Thesis
- Evidence
- Elaboration
- Realism
- Narrative elements

Strand 3: Critiquing Text

- Believability, Author's intent
- Common elements of the genre
- Individual rights vs. common good (SS connection/application of SS concepts)
- Protagonist (realistic fiction v. scifi/speculative fiction)
- Appeal
- Brainwashing vs. awareness
- Text evidence
- Connotation

Unit Title: *Dystopian Societies: Could this really be our future?* **Conceptual Lens:** Theme/Critical Analysis
Grade Level: 8

Generalizations	Guiding Questions: F=Factual; C=Conceptual; D=Debatable
1. A theme of a story develops over the course of the text through the interaction and relationships of the characters, setting, and plot.	1a. What is the theme of your text? How do you know? (F) 1b. What happened in the beginning, middle, and end of the story to help you understand the theme? (F) 1c. What details or references helped to deepen your understanding of the theme of the story? (F) 1d. How do authors develop the theme of a story? (C) 1e. What is the relationship between a story's characters and setting? (for example, the impact of setting on the choices a character can make) (C) 1f. What is the relationship between a story's characters and the plot? (for example, how interactions among characters drive plot) (C)
2. Dystopian stories explore a unique question or dilemma about the universal human experience.	2a. What are universal human experiences? (F) 2b. What experiences of the characters in the text ____ seem to be universal human experiences? (F) 2c. How is dystopian literature similar or different from realistic fiction? (F) 2d. What elements do you notice in your novel that seem unique to this genre? (F) 2e. How does literature provide insight into the universal human experience, and the social realities of the world? (C) 2f. Why are dystopian novels so popular with young adults? (D)
3. Readers discover the negative elements of a dystopian society through connections with the struggles of a protagonist.	*Initial focus on development of an understanding of the "negative" elements of dystopian societies.* 3a. What is utopia? What is a dystopia? (F) 3b. How are dystopias created, or how do they come to be? (F) 3c. What are negative elements of a society? What are the negative elements of the society in your text? (F) 3d. What is societal control? What are examples of societal control? (F) 3e. What is the relationship between societal control and conflict/choices? (C) 3f. What makes a society good or bad? (D) *Focus on the reader making sense of text.* 3g. What particular lines of dialogue or incidents in a story created connections between you and the struggles of the protagonist? (F) 3h. What are common struggles of protagonists in dystopian literature? (C) 3i. How do connections with the struggles of a story's protagonist help a reader discover the negative elements of a dystopian society? (C)
4. Collaborative deep text analysis supports the recognition and grasp of allusions by providing new insights and extending understanding.	4a. What is deep analysis of a text? (F) 4b. What strategies are important when collaborating with others in deep text analysis? (F) 4c. What is an allusion? (F) 4d. How does an author's use of allusions change reading expectations? (C) 4e. How can collaborative deep text analysis help uncover meaning that may have been previously unnoticed? (C) 4f. How can collaborative deep text analysis provide new insights and extend understanding? (C) 4g. Why do some texts lend themselves to collaborative deep analysis more than others? (C) 4h. What are the potential consequences of not deeply analyzing complex text? (D)

(Continued)

(Continued)

5. Text-based evidence strengthens the credibility of literary analysis.	5a. What is literary analysis? (F) 5b. What are some strategies for deepening the analysis in my writing? (F) 5c. How can evidence strengthen the credibility of literary analysis? (F) 5d. How does a lack of explicit text evidence affect a literary analysis? (C) 5e. How can writers ensure a literary analysis essay is effective? (C)
6. The believability of science-speculative fiction stories increases when the new world contains a blend of realistic and unrealistic elements.	6a. What are realistic details? (F) 6b. In the scene ____, which details about the setting are realistic and which are unrealistic? Explain. (F) 6c. What do the details of the setting in your text help you understand about the new world? (F) 6d. How does an author of dystopian literature create or develop a new world reality? (C) 6e. How does an author makes a science-speculative fiction story believable? (C) 6f. How much of a new world, depicted in dystopian literature, can be unrealistic yet still be believable for you as the reader? (D)
7. Authors of dystopian literature craft worst-case scenarios to cause readers to critique society's values.	7a. What are societal values? (F) 7b. What societal value is the author of your novel critiquing? How can you tell? (F) 7c. What is the relationship between the societal values explored in your novel and the societal values reflected in an historic or current political situation? (F) 7d. Why do authors of dystopian literature depict a worst-case scenario of a society? (C) 7e. Why do authors write dystopian literature? (D)

Critical Content and Key Skills

Critical Content by Strands	Key Skills
Students will know . . .	**Students will be able to . . .**
Strand 1: Understanding Text • Elements of a dystopian society • Definition of societal values • Negative aspects of society • Setting or time frame of the story • Theme of the story • Types of and responses to societal control: corruption, oppression, fear, manipulation, survival, hope, rebellion, • Inference • Conflict in the story • Definition of allusion • Strategies for deep text analysis	CCSS.ELA-LITERACY.RL.8.1: Cite the textual evidence that most strongly supports an analysis of what the text says explicitly as well as inferences drawn from the text. CCSS.ELA-LITERACY.RL.8.2: Determine a theme or central idea of a text and analyze its development over the course of the text, including its relationship to the characters, setting, and plot; provide an objective summary of the text. CCSS.ELA-LITERACY.RL.8.3: Analyze how particular lines of dialogue or incidents in a story or drama propel the action, reveal aspects of a character, or provoke a decision. CCSS.ELA-LITERACY.RL.8.9: Analyze how a modern work of fiction draws on themes, patterns of events, or character types from myths, traditional stories, or religious works such as the Bible, including describing how the material is rendered new.
Strand 2: Responding to Text • Collaborative discussion protocols • Types of reader connections • Qualities of personal reflection • Influence • Perspectives; interpretation • Probing questions	CCSS.ELA-LITERACY.SL.8.1.A: Come to discussions prepared, having read or researched material under study; explicitly draw on that preparation by referring to evidence on the topic, text, or issue to probe and reflect on ideas under discussion. CCSS.ELA-LITERACY.SL.8.1B: Follow rules for collegial discussions and decision making, track progress toward specific goals and deadlines, and define individual roles as needed. CCSS.ELA-LITERACY.SL.8.1C: Pose questions that connect the ideas of several speakers and respond to others' questions and comments with relevant evidence, observations, and ideas. CCSS.ELA-LITERACY.SL.8.1D: Acknowledge new information expressed by others, and, when warranted, qualify or justify their own views in light of the evidence presented.
Strand 3: Critiquing Text • Traits of believability • Author's intent • Connotation • Common elements of the genre • Protagonist (realistic fiction vs. scifi/speculative fiction) • Appeal to readers • Key vocabulary related to dystopia: Brainwashing vs. awareness	CCSS.ELA-LITERACY.RL.8.4: Determine the meaning of words and phrases as they are used in a text, including figurative and connotative meanings; analyze the impact of specific word choices on meaning and tone, including analogies or allusions to other texts. CCSS.ELA-LITERACY.L.8.5: Demonstrate understanding of figurative language, word relationships, and nuances in word meanings. CCSS.ELA-LITERACY.W.8.1: Write arguments to support claims with clear reasons and relevant evidence.

(Continued)

(Continued)

Strand 4: Producing Text • Writing process • Process of literary analysis • Claim • Text evidence • Elaboration • Realism • Narrative elements • Quality narrative writing techniques	CCSS.ELA-LITERACY.W.8.1A: Introduce claim(s), acknowledge and distinguish the claim(s) from alternate or opposing claims, and organize the reasons and evidence logically. CCSS.ELA-LITERACY.W.8.1B: Support claim(s) with logical reasoning and relevant evidence, using accurate, credible sources and demonstrating an understanding of the topic or text. CCSS.ELA-LITERACY.W.8.1C: Use words, phrases, and clauses to create cohesion and clarify the relationships among claim(s), counterclaims, reasons, and evidence. CCSS.ELA-LITERACY.W.8.1E: Provide a concluding statement or section that follows from and supports the argument presented. CCSS.ELA-LITERACY.W.8.3A-E: Write narratives to develop real or imagined experiences or events using effective technique, relevant descriptive details, and well-structured event sequences.

Unit Title: *Dystopian Societies: Could this really be our future?*
Grade Level: 8

Suggested Time Line	Suggested Learning Experiences (Note: G#=Target Generalization)	Assessments	Differentiation	Resources

Thinking About Learning Experiences

Now that you have learned about lesson design, analyzed several model lessons, and explored a variety of Concept-Based Literacy Classroom Snapshots, how would you. . .

- structure and sequence the learning experiences to guide students to the unit generalizations and prepare them for the end of unit assessment?
- support opportunities for inquiry and conceptual thinking?
- differentiate to ensure equitable access for all learners?
- continually assess students' developing knowledge, skills, and understandings?

Culminating Unit Assessment

Unit Title: *Dystopian Societies: Could this really be our future?* **Conceptual Lens:** Theme/Critical Analysis
Grade Level: 8

Option 1: What (the unit focus): Students will investigate dystopian societies,

Why (the generalization or generalizations): in order to understand that . . .

Authors of dystopian literature craft worst-case scenarios to cause readers to critique society's values.

How (the engaging scenario for students):

How are you feeling after reading the oppressive picture your authors created of a potential future state? Are you ready to move on to utopian literature? Before we turn our reading to happier thoughts, you have a final assessment to complete.

Based on the dystopian novel you read, your final task is to write a literary analysis essay. Your analysis should include the following:

- the theme of your novel,
- how the author developed that theme from worst-case scenarios over the course of the text,
- and, finally, how the author caused you, the reader, to critique societal values based on the worst-case scenarios.

Make sure you cite specific evidence from the text to support your analysis.

Option 2: *Alternate Culminating Assessment With a Narrative Writing Focus*

How (the engaging scenario):

How are you feeling after reading the oppressive picture your authors created of a potential future state? Think about our current society. What societal value or issue would you like to explore as a worst-case scenario? Identify a news article representing a societal value or issue. Think about the message or theme you would like to communicate to your reader. Using the things you uncovered in this unit about how author's craft dystopian literature, write a short story inspired by your news article. Follow a formal writing process, including peer review.

Upon completion of your short story, complete a craft report reflecting on:

- how your story reflects the value or issue from your news article.
- the choices you made as an author of dystopian literature to communicate your theme.

Support your reflection with specific examples from your story.

---

* Create a new scoring guide to align with this variation.

Scoring Guide

4 Meets and exceeds standard criteria.

3

STANDARD

Highlight descriptors that are met

Understanding

Literary analysis essay explains how the author caused the reader to critique society's values with sufficient detail to demonstrate conceptual understanding (of the target generalization).

Content

- Essay communicates the theme of the novel
- Provides specific evidence from the novel that shows the author's position on the societal value(s) critiqued in the novel

Process

Literary Analysis Essay:

- Effective introduction: hooks reader, and claim is clearly communicated
- Provides thorough and convincing support/evidence for the argument(s) and claim that includes the effective use of sources (facts and details)
- Demonstrates effective use of elaborative techniques
- Focus is strongly maintained for the purpose, audience, and task
- Transitions help build logical progression of ideas
- Clearly and effectively expresses ideas, using precise language
- Essay has substantial depth and thoroughly explains the thesis
- Sources are smoothly integrated and properly cited
- Conclusion effectively wraps up the essay and leaves the reader with something to think about
- Reflects a formal style
- Demonstrates command of grade level grammar and conventions

* *Language from Smarter Balanced Assessment Scoring Rubrics*

2 Meets 7/11 of the criteria in the Process standard. Meets 1/2 of the criteria in the Content standard. Meets the Understanding standard.

1 Non-scorable: Does not yet approach standard

Resource A-4 Grade 7 *Every Voice Counts: The Struggle for Equity*

Grade Level: 7
Unit Number: 1

Unit Title: *Every Voice Counts: The struggle for equity* **Conceptual Lens:** Communication/Clarity

Unit Length: Approximately 9–10 weeks

Authors: Adapted from unit created by Nolan Harron, Helen Hollister, Jim Palmer, Burlington-Edison School District, Burlington, Washington, USA

Unit Overview:

Here is a question: "How can I use my voice to raise awareness of important issues?" As a middle schooler, your heart is full of compassion, you love to help others, and you have so many ideas to share. In this unit you will explore the relationship between effective communication and clarity as you learn about struggles for equity around the world, including access to education, water, shelter, food, family and love, and economic opportunities. You will form inquiry groups around a specific equity issue. Each week you will read and analyze resources to build understanding of your topic, while gaining a deeper understanding of the qualities and characteristics of texts that clearly communicate information for the reader. In this unit, you will be able to talk—a lot! You will participate in academic conversations both in your inquiry groups and as a whole class. Our investigation will culminate by demonstrating your understanding of the key concepts through the creation of a digital magazine to teach others about your issue. Our digital magazines will be posted online so that you can communicate your ideas with our community, and maybe even the world!

Technology Integration:

- Digital Collaboration on Writing
- Web-based research
- Creation of charts, graphs, and visuals
- Design and layout for digital magazines

Standards or national curricula addressed in this unit:

CCSS.ELA-LITERACY.RI.7.1
CCSS.ELA-LITERACY.RI.7.2
CCSS.ELA-LITERACY.RI.7.5
CCSS.ELA-LITERACY.RI.7.9
CCSS.ELA-LiTERACY.W.7.2
CCSS.ELA-LITERACY.W.7.2A
CCSS.ELA-LITERACY.W.7.2B
CCSS.ELA-LITERACY.W.7.2C
CCSS.ELA-LITERACY.W.7.8
CCSS.ELALITERACY.SL.7.1
CCSS.ELA-LITERACY.SL.7.1B
CCSS.ELA-LITERACY.SL.7.1C
CCSS.ELA-LITERACY.SL.7.1D
CCSS.ELA-LITERACY.SL.7.2
CCSS.ELA-LITERACY.SL.7.5
CCCSS.ELA-LITERACY.L.7.4A

Unit Title: *Every Voice Counts: The struggle for equity* **Conceptual Lens:** Communication/Clarity
Grade Level: 7

Strand 1: Understanding Text

- Central idea
- Supporting details
- Summary
- Organization
- Text Structure (for example, cause-effect, comparison/contrast)
- Text Features and Formatting (for example, headings), graphics (charts, tables, illustrations, and so on)
- Inference
- Context Clues
- Evidence
- Author's Purpose

Strand 2: Responding to Text

- Questions
- Observations
- Clear Communication
- Point of View
- Reflections
- Appropriate feedback
- Socratic seminar procedures
- Elaboration
- Collaboration
- Connections

Unit Title:

Every Voice Counts

Strand 4: Producing Text

- Explanatory Organization
- Relevant Content
- Topic Sentence
- Closing Sentence
- Details
- Elaboration
- Text Structure
- Text Features and Formatting
- Transitions
- Audience Awareness
- Clarity
- Research

Strand 3: Critiquing Text

- Emphasis
- Point of View
- Fact vs. Fiction
- Effective Text Structure
- Author's Craft
- Source
- Credibility
- Currency
- Relevance
- Accuracy
- Value of Multimedia

Unit Title: *Every Voice Counts: The struggle for equity* **Conceptual Lens:** Communication/Clarity
Grade Level: 7

Generalizations	Guiding Questions: F=Factual; C=Conceptual; D=Debatable
1. Effective communication enables others to clearly understand important issues.	1a. What is effective communication? (F) 1b. What are the elements of effective communication (informed voices, clarity of message)? (F) 1c. What does it mean to be informed? (F) 1d. How can informed voices teach others? (C) 1e. What is the relationship between effective communication and audience understanding? (C) 1f. What happens when writing or a presentation is not clear? (C) 1g. How should people be held responsible for accurate and effective communication of important ideas? (D)
2. Readers analyze the development of the central idea of a text to create an objective summary.	2a. What is the central idea(s) of your text? Support with evidence. (F) 2b. What reading strategies helped you determine the central idea(s)? (F) 2c. How did the author of your article develop the central idea(s) across the text? (F) 2d. What is an "objective summary" of text? (F) 2e. What skills support crafting an objective summary of a text? (F) 2f. How does analyzing how the central idea(s) of text is developed vs. simply identifying the central ideas(s) help ensure a summary will be objective? (C) 2g. Why are objective summaries of text important? (C)
3. Discourse enables participants to revise and deepen their current understanding of a topic, idea, or concept.	3a. What does a respectful conversation look like and sound like? (F) 3b. What did someone say during your group conversation that caused you to think differently about the topic? (F) 3c. What role does discourse play in understanding a text? (C) 3d. Why is it necessary to revise thinking? (C) 3e. Do we always have to accept the ideas of others? (D)
4. Researchers assess the credibility and accuracy of sources to ensure the information is reliable.	4a. What makes a source credible? (F) 4b. Does ___ (source) provide reliable information? How can you tell? (F) 4c. How do researchers determine if a source of information is reliable? (C) 4d. Why is it important to use information from only reliable sources in research papers? (C) 4e. What is the relationship among credibility, accuracy, and reliability? (C)
5. Writers select a text structure and specific text features that will most clearly convey ideas for the reader.	5a. What are examples of different types of text structures? (F) 5b. What are examples of different types of text features? (F) 5c. What text structure did _____ (author) use to organize information and ideas? (F) 5d. Which text features did this author use? (F) 5e. What impact did the text structure and features have for you as the reader? (F) 5f. How is the organization of informational texts different than other types of writing? (C) 5g. How do writers of informational texts decide how to best structure their writing to effectively convey ideas? (C) 5h. What is the relationship between text features and communicating ideas with clarity? (C)

6. Writers develop topics with relevant facts, definitions, concrete details, quotations, or other information and examples to support ideas and to add precision of thought.	6a. What techniques did the author of ____ (text) use to develop the topic? [relevant facts, definitions, concrete details, quotations, examples, and so on] (F) 6b. What is "precision of thought"? (F) 6c. How does a writer's development of a topic add support for the ideas and precision of thought ? (F) 6d. Why is it important for writers to develop topics well? (C) 6e. What happens when writers do not strategically develop topics? (D)
7. Presenters include multimedia components and visual displays to clarify information, support claims, and emphasize salient points.	7a. What do you notice about the use of multimedia in the presentation? (F) 7b. What is the purpose of the multimedia? (F) 7c. How do presenters determine the most effective multimedia to use? (C) 7d. What role does a presenter's choice in multimedia play in achieving his/her purpose? (C)
8. Respecting and embracing the voices of all people will help address worldwide struggles for equity.	8a. What is equity? (F) 8b. What are some of the universal struggles for equity? (F) 8c. How can technology advances and globalization help and hinder worldwide equity? (C) 8d. How do voices become marginalized in different cultures? (C) 8e. Does being equitable mean everyone should be able to get the same thing? (D)

Critical Content and Key Skills

Critical Content by Strands	Key Skills
Students will know. . .	**Students will be able to. . .**
Strand 1: Understanding Text • Key vocabulary: strive and thrive • Types of Text Structures (cause-effect, comparison/contrast, and so on) • Types Text Features and Formatting (headings, bold face print, italic text, glossary, and so on.), graphics (charts, tables, illustrations, and so on) • Value of context clues	CCSS.ELA-LITERACY.RI.7.1: Cite several pieces of textual evidence to support analysis of what the text says explicitly as well as inferences drawn from the text. CCSS.ELA-LITERACY.RI.7.2: Determine two or more central ideas in a text and analyze their development over the course of the text; provide an objective summary of the text. CCSS.ELA-LITERACY.RI.7.5: Analyze the structure an author uses to organize a text, including how the major sections contribute to the whole and to the development of the ideas. CCSS.ELA-LITERACY.L.7.4A: Use context (e.g., the overall meaning of a sentence or paragraph; a word's position or function in a sentence) as a clue to the meaning of a word or phrase.
Strand 2: Responding to Text • Procedures of collegial Socratic discussions • Relevant and different types of questions • Sentence starters to provoke elaboration • Strategies for collaboration • Guidelines for appropriate feedback	CCSS.ELA-LITERACY.SL.7.1B: Follow rules for collegial discussions, track progress toward specific goals and deadlines, and define individual roles as needed. CCSS.ELA-LITERACY.SL.7.1C: Pose questions that elicit elaboration and respond to others' questions and comments with relevant observations and ideas that bring the discussion back on topic as needed. CCSS.ELA-LITERACY.SL.7.1D: Acknowledge new information expressed by others and, when warranted, modify their own views.
Strand 3: Critiquing Text • Techniques for evaluating sources • Strengths of different modes of communication • Value of various presentation media formats and visuals	CCSS.ELA-LITERACY.RI.7.9: Analyze how two or more authors writing about the same topic shape their presentations of key information by emphasizing different evidence or advancing different interpretations of facts. CCSS.ELA-LITERACY.SL.7.2: Analyze the main ideas and supporting details presented in diverse media and formats (e.g., visually, quantitatively, orally) and explain how the ideas clarify a topic, text, or issue under study. CCSS.ELA-LITERACY.W.7.8: Gather relevant information from multiple print and digital sources, using search terms effectively; assess the credibility and accuracy of each source; and quote or paraphrase the data and conclusions of others while avoiding plagiarism and following a standard format for citation.

Strand 4: Producing Text • Tools for multimedia integration • Transition words and phrases • Relevant facts, concrete details, and so on • Different text structures/features for informational texts	CCSS.ELA-LITERACY.W.7.2: Write informative/explanatory texts to examine a topic and convey ideas, concepts, and information through the selection, organization, and analysis of relevant content. CCSS.ELA-LITERACY.W.7.2A: Introduce a topic clearly, previewing what is to follow; organize ideas, concepts, and information, using strategies such as definition, classification, comparison/contrast, and cause/effect; include formatting (for example, headings), graphics (for example, charts, tables), and multimedia when useful to aiding comprehension. CCSS.ELA-LITERACY.W.7.2B: Develop the topic with relevant facts, definitions, concrete details, quotations, or other information and examples. CCSS.ELA-LITERACY.W.7.2C: Use appropriate transitions to create cohesion and clarify the relationships among ideas and concepts. CCSS.ELA-LITERACY.SL.7.5: Include multimedia components and visual displays in presentations to clarify claims and findings and emphasize salient points.

Unit Title: *Every Voice Counts: The struggle for equity* **Conceptual Lens:** Communication/Clarity
Grade Level: 7

Suggested Timeline	Suggested Learning Experiences	Assessments	Differentiation	Resources

Thinking About Learning Experiences

In Model Unit 2, *Dystopian Societies: Could this really be our future?*, we asked you to consider the following questions:

How would you. . .

- structure and sequence the learning experiences to guide students to the unit generalizations and prepare them for the end of unit assessment?
- differentiate to ensure equitable access for all learners?
- assess students' knowledge, skills and understandings?

Now, let's take our thinking one step further.

If you were to create learning experiences for this unit, how would you balance the process of learning through inductive inquiry with explicit skill instruction?

- What knowledge, skills, and understanding would best be taught through inquiry?
- What would best be taught through explicit instruction in the context of the ongoing inquiry?
- Are there skills, content, or concepts in which you would Pause & Zoom-in?
- How will you use the ongoing inquiry to create a sense of urgency, relevance, or timeliness for the upcoming explicit instruction?

Culminating Unit Assessment

Unit Title: *Every Voice Counts: The struggle for equity* **Conceptual Lens:** Communication/Clarity
Grade Level: 7

What (the unit focus): Students will investigate how voices count in the struggle for equity,

Why (the generalization or generalizations): in order to understand that . . .

- Presenters include multimedia components and visual displays to clarify information, support claims, and emphasize salient points.
- Respecting and embracing the voices of all people will help address worldwide struggles for equity.

How (the engaging scenario for students):

Working in teams, you will create an educational digital magazine. The magazine will contain articles, images, charts, visuals, and whatever else you choose to use to educate your audience about the issue related to struggles for equity around the world that you selected. Each group will publish one article with at least one supporting multimedia component.

Examples of Struggles for Equity

- Access to Education
- Access to Family and Love
- Access to Water
- Access to Food
- Access to Shelter
- Access to Economic Opportunities

Digital magazines will be posted on a public webpage to reach a broad audience.

After your publication is posted, you will individually write a 3-paragraph craft report explaining:

- how the multimedia components and visual displays helped clarify information about your worldwide equity issue,
- how the multimedia components and visual displays helped support your claim about your worldwide equity issue, and
- how the multimedia components and visual displays helped emphasize your salient points about respecting and embracing all people's voices.

Scoring Guide

For Letter Grades

Possible Pts. or % | Self-Assess. | Teacher Assess.

Scoring Criteria

S T A N D A R D

Understanding:

Content:

Process:

Scoring Ke[y]
A =
B =
C =
I =

Thinking About Scoring Guides

Model Unit 1, *Language As a Tool of Persuasion*, and Model Unit 2, *Dystopian Societies: Could this really be our future?* provide two different examples of scoring tools for the culminating assessment. These examples are alternatives to a traditional rubric. Each example is multidimensional, demystifies evaluation for students, and provides teachers with consistency in assessing students' learning.

Language As a Tool of Persuasion shows a scoring guide that is based on 100 possible points, which translates easily into a letter grade system. The scoring guide also allows for both student self-assessment, and teacher assessment on the same paper. This is a powerful way to cultivate a collaborative relationship between the teacher and student as learning partners.

Dystopian Societies: Could this really be our future? shows a scoring guide based on a 4-point scale. This type supports standards-based grading systems. In the process section, language expectations for evaluating the traits of student writing are described clearly, targeting specific writing techniques.

Both units provide examples of Concept-Based scoring guides that evaluate three-dimensional learning: What students ***K****now* (content), *Understand* (generalization), *and are able to* ***D****o* (process/strategies/skills), at the end of the curriculum unit. This differs from two-dimensional scoring guides that assess only knowledge about a topic and/or a student's ability to demonstrate a skill. Assessing the three dimensions separately allows scoring to be tailored to a specific unit and gives flexibility in emphasis.

Now it's your turn! Reread the Culminating Assessment for this unit, Every Voice Counts: The Struggle for Equity. If you were to create a scoring guide for this assessment, what criteria or descriptors would you include to measure what students . . . ***K****now,* ***U****nderstand, and are be able to* ***D****o (or, the KUDs)?*

Resource A-5 Grade 9 *Oh, the Choices Authors Face!*

Grade Level: 9

Unit Number: 2

Unit Title: *Oh The Choices Authors Face!* **Conceptual Lens:** Author's Craft/Choice

Unit Length: Approximately 4–6 weeks

Unit Overview:

Oh the choices authors face! Oh the places those choices can take us! Think about all the choices authors make about the characters, plot, setting, language, organization, genre, details, references . . . the list goes on. In this unit, we are going to investigate some of the distinct choices authors make. Sometimes their choices create a more interesting piece. Sometimes the choices cause readers to pause, wonder, or struggle to understand. Sometimes choices push the margins on convention and ethics. Authors are our writing mentors. As you analyze their choices, you are expanding your personal repertoire of writing choices. Finally, at our Community Open House this year, you will be showcasing the choices you make as an author!

Technology Integration:

- Digital media
- Word Processing

Standards or national curricula addressed in this unit:

CCSS.ELA-LITERACY.RL.9-10.4
CCSS.ELA.LITERACY.RL9-10.5
CCSS.ELA-LITERACY.RL.9-10.7
CCSS.ELA-LITERACY.RI9-10.7
CCSS.ELA-LITERACY.W.9-10.4
CCSS.ELA-LITERACY.W.9-10.6
CCSS.ELA-LITERACY.SL.9-10.1.A
CCSS.ELA-LITERACY.SL.9-10.1d
CCSS.ELA-LITERACY.L.8.3

Unit Title: *Oh The Choices Authors Face!* **Conceptual Lens:** Author's Craft/Choice
Grade Level: 9

Strand 1: Understanding Text

- Reading strategies
- Author's purpose
- Elements of writer's craft:
    - Word choice
    - Style
    - Text medium
    - Text structure
    - Text type (genre)
    - Surprise
    - Literary devices

Strand 2: Responding to Text

- Clear goals
- Respect for differences
- Reflection
- Evidence
- Individual and group responsibilities
- Connections
- Collaboration

Unit Title:

Oh The Choices Authors Face!

Strand 4: Producing Text

- Writing conventions
- Language in different contexts
- Nuances in word meaning
- Medium and message
- Various mediums
- Tone
- Purpose

Strand 3: Critiquing Text

- Effectiveness of author's choices:
    - Medium
    - Style
    - Word choice
- Strength of message
- Literary/creative license
- Audience impact
- Contradictions
- Evidence

Unit Title: *Oh The Choices Authors Face!* **Conceptual Lens:** Author's Craft/Choice
Grade Level: 9

Generalizations	Guiding Questions: F=Factual; C=Conceptual; D=Debatable
1. Authors make choices that shape how an audience receives, responds to, and understands the text.	1a. What are some of the factors that direct the choices an author will make? (F) [genre, audience, purpose, topic, and so on] 1b. What are some common choices authors make about their writing? (F) 1c. What choices did your author make that required more of your focused attention to make sense of the text? (F) 1d. What did your author do that helped you receive or understand his/her message? What was your response? [explain using text evidence] (F) 1e. How do an author's choices impact an audience? (C) 1f. Why is it important for authors to understand the relationship between writing choices and audience? (C) 1g. Why do authors make the choices they do? (D)
2. Reading/viewing strategies and an understanding of writer's craft help uncover and explain the choices an author makes.	2a. What reading strategies did you use to make sense of a motif in *Beloved* by T. Morrison? (F) 2b. What are some viewing strategies that help an audience see the choices an author made in a visual communication? (F) 2b. How can knowledge of writer's craft support an analysis of an author's choices? (C) 2c. How can analyzing the choices an author makes enhance one's own writing craft? (C)
3. Collaboration expands the thinking and the generation of new ideas for each participant.	3a. What does collaboration look like, sound like, feel like? (F) 3b. What factors causes collaboration to fail? (F) 3c. Why is collaboration valuable to everyone involved? (C) 3d. How does collaboration differ from cooperation? (C) 3e. What was one thing someone in your group said or did that expanded your thinking? (D)
4. An author's purpose, audience, and message direct the best choice of communication medium.	4a. What are examples of different types of communication mediums? (F) 4b. What details of the subject _____are represented in the first medium example (for example print)? What details remain the same or change when this same subject is represented in a different medium (for example, video clip)? (F) 4c. How do different mediums shape how a subject is represented? (C) 4d. How is an author's purpose reflected his/her choice of medium? (C) 4e. Can one medium be relied on more than another to accurately represent a subject? (D)
5. Technology can expand an author's reach of audience and enhance the strength of the message.	5a. What are the characteristics of digital media that grab an audience's attention? (F) 5b. Which technologies aid your writing? (F) 5b. How can technology expand an author's audience? (C) 5c. How can technology tools enhance or dilute an author's message? (C) 5b. Why has visual literacy become so universal? (C)

Critical Content and Key Skills

Critical Content by Strands	Key Skills
Students will know . . .	**Students will be able to . . .**
Strand 1: Understanding Text • Elements of writer's craft/various writing techniques • Effective reading strategies • Author's purpose	CCSS.ELA-LITERACY.RL.9-10.4: Determine the meaning of words and phrases as they are used in a text, including figurative, connotative, and technical meanings; analyze the cumulative impact of specific word choices on meaning and tone.
Strand 2: Responding to Text • Protocols for effective discussions • Group member responsibilities • Requirements for collaboration	CCSS.ELA-LITERACY.SL.9-10.1.A: Come to discussions prepared, having read and researched material under study; explicitly draw on that preparation by referring to evidence from texts and other research on the topic or issue to stimulate a thoughtful, well-reasoned exchange of ideas. CCSS.ELA-LITERACY.SL.9-10.1D: Respond thoughtfully to diverse perspectives, summarize points of agreement and disagreement, and, when warranted, qualify or justify their own views and understanding and make new connections in light of the evidence and reasoning presented.
Strand 3: Critiquing Text • Impact of the different choices authors make • Message strength and clarity • Effect of different types of medium	CCSS.ELA-LITERACY.RL.9-10.7: Analyze the representation of a subject or a key scene in two different artistic mediums, including what is emphasized or absent in each treatment). CCSS.ELA-LITERACY.RI.9-10.7:Analyze various accounts of a subject told in different mediums (for example, a person's life story in both print and multimedia), determining which details are emphasized in each account. CCSS.ELA-LITERACY.RL9-10.5: Analyze how an author's choices concerning how to structure a text, order events within it (for example, parallel plots), and manipulate time (for example, pacing, flashbacks) creates such effects as mystery, tension, or surprise.
Strand 4: Producing Text • Various technology tools • Qualities of clear, coherent writing • Audience • Language conventions in different mediums	CCSS.ELA-LITERACY.W.9-10.6: Use technology, including the Internet, to produce, publish, and update individual or shared writing products, taking advantage of technology's capacity to link to other information and to display information flexibly and dynamically. CCSS.ELA-LITERACY.W.9-10.4: Produce clear and coherent writing in which the development, organization, and style are appropriate to task, purpose, and audience. CCSS.ELA-LITERACY.L.8.3: Use knowledge of language and its conventions when writing, speaking, reading, or listening.

Unit Title: *Oh The Choices Authors Face!* **Conceptual Lens:** Author's Craft/Choice
Grade Level: 9

Suggested Timeline	Suggested Learning Experiences	Assessments	Differentiation	Resources

Thinking About Learning Experiences

In Model Unit 3, *Every Voice Counts: The struggle for equity,* we asked you to consider the balance of teaching through inductive inquiry and explicit skill instruction.

You reflected on the following questions:

If you were to create learning experiences for this unit, how would you balance the process of learning through inductive inquiry with explicit skill instruction?

- What knowledge, skills, and understanding would best be taught through inquiry?
- What would best be taught through explicit instruction in the context of the ongoing inquiry?
- Are there skills, content, or concepts in which you would Pause-Zoom-in?
- How will you use the ongoing inquiry to create a sense of urgency, relevance, or timeliness for the upcoming explicit instruction?

Now let's think about this. . .

Knowing that the gradual release of responsibility and ownership for learning from the teacher to the student is a pillar of any balanced literacy classroom, how would you ensure that this is a foundational element of this unit?

- What skill, strategy, or type of problem solving would best be taught through the gradual release of responsibility?
- What piece of mentor text or example that reflects the learning target could be used to model, by thinking aloud, the skill, strategy, or type of problem solving that students would be expected to utilize in their upcoming learning experience?
- How will you know when students are ready for independent practice?

Culminating Unit Assessment

Unit Title: *Oh The Choices Authors Face!* **Conceptual Lens:** Author's Craft/Choice
Grade Level: 9

What (the unit focus): Students will investigate the consequences of an author's choices.

Why (the generalization or generalizations): Authors make choices that shape how an audience receives, responds to, and understands the text.

How (the engaging scenario for students):

You have read an amazing number of different types of texts in this unit. The mini-inquiries about the choices authors make uncovered some fascinating theories about why a choice may have been made and the impact it had on you as readers, viewers, or listeners. A theme of different "isms" ran across much of the content in the different mediums of texts (print and nonprint) you analyzed. For example, racism, activism, altruism, sexism, sizeism, volunteerism. I have put together an assorted list of short texts that address a variety of -isms. Now it is your turn to impact an audience!

You will create a piece that makes a statement about an –ism that resonates with you to be showcased in our community open house. What is in your heart? What is your intended result? How will you communicate that with your audience? What craft choices will you make as an author? We've explored classic literature, poetry, art, photography, and so much more in this unit. What medium will you choose to bring your message about your –ism to life?

Here is your final assessment:

Part 1:

1. Select and read a short text or excerpt about an "-ism" that resonates with you.
2. Notice a specific craft choice the author of your text made.
3. Talk about the choice with a writing peer and brainstorm why the author may have made this choice and how this choice shaped your reaction to and understanding of the text. Record your thinking in #1 of your 4-part Reflection Sheet, which will be turned in at the end of the week.
4. Give the craft a name and record it on your Reflection Sheet (#2).
5. Think of other examples of where you have seen this craft used and record your response (#3).

Part 2:

6. Create your piece for the community open house. Make craft choices and choose your medium based on your purpose and on the audience. Also, think of a creative title that captures the essence of your piece.
7. On #4 of your Reflection Sheet, share how you used craft choice(s) to shape how your audience would receive, respond to, and understand your message. (Self-assess using the class rubric.)

Scoring Guide

	Exceeding Expectations (4)	Meeting Expectations (3)	Not yet, but I will! (2)
Understanding			
Process			
Content			

Thinking About Scoring Guides

In the Thinking About Scoring Guides section for Model Unit 3, *Every Voice Counts: The Struggle for Equity,* you learned that Concept-Based scoring guides always include assessment of Understanding, Process, and Content. You also learned that the format of the scoring guide can be created for a points-based or a standards-based reporting system. The trick here is to create a scoring guide that works within your unique system at your school while still providing valuable feedback about a students' Understanding, Process, and Content.

Here's another variation. For this scoring guide, the teacher would only fill in descriptors for the *Meeting Expectations* column. This clearly defines what students would know, understand, and be able to do in order to meet expectations. By leaving the other two columns, *Exceeding Expectations and Not yet, but I will!,* blank, the teacher can provide feedback specific to the individual student. If we want to create Culminating Assessment without a ceiling or cap for exceeding the expectations, then the scoring guide must not try to define what *Exceeding Expectations* looks like. Can we really predict all the ways that students might move beyond Meeting Expectations?

The intentional use of the language of *Not yet, but I will!* captures the spirit of being growth minded, helping students see that while they did not yet meet the expectation, they will. Leaving this column blank allows the teacher to provided individualized feedback about what the student can do to move closer to meeting the expectations.

Now it's your turn! Thinking about the Culminating Assessment in this unit, *Oh The Choices Authors Face!,* what type of Scoring Guide would you create? Why did you choose this type over another?

Score: _____/4

1- Not Enough work provided to score

Resource A-6 Grade 4 *Personal Narratives: Here's My Story*

Grade Level: 5

Unit Number: 1

Unit Title: *Personal Narratives: Here's My Story*

Conceptual Lens: Genre/Author's Craft

Unit Length: Approximately 8–10 weeks

Unit Overview:

Have you ever told a really funny story only to realize that you are the only one laughing? Nobody else got the story! Oh snap . . . I guess you had to be there. How do authors, who share personal stories, help readers "be there" through their craft and choice in words? How do these authors help readers see the point of their story? In this unit, we will explore the relationship between effective personal narratives and the craft behind the story. We are going to dig in and think about how you, as the central character in your personal narrative, can create stories that capture the hearts and imaginations of readers. Through your story, you are going to learn how to make the reader laugh with you, cry with you, or whatever else you choose. Get ready to take a trip down memory lane!

Technology Integration:

- Word processing
- Collaborative writing through Google Docs

Standards or national curricula addressed in this unit:

CCSS.ELA-LITERACY.RL.5.1
CCSS.ELA-LITERACY.RL.5.2
CCSS.ELA-LITERACY.RL.5.6
CCSS.ELA-LITERACY.RL.5.9
CCSS.ELA-LITERACY.W.5.1C
CCSS.ELA-LITERACY.W.5.3
CCSS.ELA-LITERACY.W.5.3A
CCSS.ELA-LITERACY.W.5.3B
CCSS.ELA-LITERACY.W.5.3A
CCSS.ELA-LITERACY.W.5.3 C
CCSS.ELA-LITERACY.W.5.3D
CCSS.ELA-LITERACY.W.5.3E
CCSS.ELA-LITERACY.SL.5.1
CCSS.ELA-LITERACY.SL.5.1BA
CCSS.ELA-LITERACY.SL.5.1C
CCSS.ELA-LITERACY.SL.5.1.D
CCSS.ELA-LITERACY.SL.5.2
CCSS.ELA-LITERACY.L.5.2
CCSS.ELA-LITERACY.L.5.3.A

Unit Title: *Personal Narratives: Here's My Story*
Grade Level: 5

Conceptual Lens: Genre/Author's Craft

Strand 1: Understanding Text

- Story elements: characters, plot, setting, conflict, resolution, and so on
- Personal narrative text structures
- Mental images/imagery
- Inference
- Word choice
- Literary devices
- Vignettes
- Theme
- Point of view
- Narrator
- Summary

Strand 2: Responding to Text

- Connections
- Academic conversations
- Reader response
- Interpretation
- Reflection
- Active listening
- Questions
- Appropriate feedback
- Precise expression
- Group responsibilities

Unit Title:

Personal Narratives: Here's My Story

Strand 4: Producing Text

- Narrative techniques
- Precise language
- Sensory details
- Word choice
- Sentence structures
- Transitional words and phrases
- Writing process

Strand 3: Critiquing Text

- Elements/techniques of personal narratives
- Effectiveness of word choice
- Qualities of author's craft
- Development of people, places, and experiences
- Language precision
- Impact
- Appeal
- Clarity

Unit Title: *Personal Narratives: Here's My Story* **Conceptual Lens:** Genre/Author's Craft
Grade Level: 5

Generalizations	Guiding Questions: F=Factual; C=Conceptual; D=Debatable
1. Authors craft personal narratives so that readers feel they shared the same experience.	1a. What was the event described in the story___? (F) 1b. How did the author share the experience with you? (F) 1c. How do details and words help readers feel they are sharing the experience an author is describing? (C) 1d. Why do people share personal stories? (C) 1e. How do readers learn through the stories of others? (C) 1f. How does an author decide on a story for his/her personal narrative? (C)
2. Readers identify a narrator's point of view to understand how the events and experiences are interpreted and described in a story.	2a. What does narrator mean? What is point of view? (F) 2b. What do you know about _(narrator)_and his/her point of view in the story___? Provide evidence to support your answer. (F) 2c. How does __(narrator)__ interpret (or think, feel, or act in response to) specific events in the story? (F) 2d. What strategies do readers use to identify a narrator's point of view? (F) 2d. How might people interpret the same event in a story differently? (C) 2e. How does a narrator's point of view affect a reader's interpretation of a story? (C) 2f. Are there two sides to every story? (D)
3. Readers quote text evidence accurately to support inferences and to construct an interpretation of a story.	3a. What does it mean to quote text evidence accurately? (F) 3b. What strategies do readers use to infer information that is not explicitly stated? (F) 3c. What inferences did you make about the character/person, setting, and events in your story? (F) 3d. Why is it important to quote text evidence accurately? (C) 3e. What is the relationship between quoting text evidence accurately and reader's interpretation? (C) 3f. Can a reader's inferences and interpretations of a story be valid if they aren't supported by text evidence? (D)
4. Posing and responding to specific questions contributes to the success of academic conversations by clarifying and gathering ideas from others.	4a. What types of questions help clarify the ideas of others? (F) 4b. What types of questions help others share their ideas? (F) 4c. What is an appropriate response to questions from others? (F) 4d. What makes academic conversations successful? (F) 4e. How do academic conversation help everyone learn? (C) 4f. How do academic conversations differ from casual conversations with friends? (C)
5. Writers craft precise images of people, places and events in a reader's mind through specific words and details.	5a. What do you notice about how ___(author) described the people, places, and events, in your story? (F) 5b. What does it mean for a writer to show vs. tell? (F) 5c. How did the author of your book appeal to readers' senses? (F) 5d. How does an author's word choice create images for readers? (C) 5e. How does a personal narrative make it easier for a writer to create precise images for readers? (C)

6. Writers use narrative techniques, such as dialogue, description, and pacing, to create an interesting and enjoyable experience for the reader.	6a. What made you connect with your story? (F) 6b. What are some different narrative techniques? (F) 6c. What narrative techniques did your author use to bring your story to life for you as a reader? (F) 6d. What did you learn through the dialogue in your story? Through the descriptions? (F) 6e. How does pacing keep a story interesting? (C) 6f. How can narrative techniques be overused in a story? (C) 6f. What makes a story enjoyable? (D)
7. Writers expand, combine, and reduce sentences to add interest, style, and meaning for readers.	7a. What did you notice about the different styles of sentence structures different authors use? (F) 7b. What does it mean to expand, combine and reduce sentences? (F) 7c. How do different styles of sentences keep an author's writing interesting? (F) 7d. How can a sentence structure support meaning for readers? (clarify an idea with examples, be concise and clear, connect different ideas, and so on) (C) 7e. Why are some authors recognized by their unique sentence style? (for example, Dr. Seuss) (C)

Critical Content and Key Skills

Critical Content by Strands	Key Skills
Students will know . . .	**Students will be able to . . .**
Strand 1: Understanding Text • Comprehension monitoring strategies • Story elements (characters, plot, setting, conflict, resolution, significant event, and so on) • Definition of point of view • Types of point of view • Different types of story structures	CCSS.ELA-LITERACY.RL.5.1: Quote accurately from a text when explaining what the text says explicitly and when drawing inferences from the text. CCSS.ELA-LITERACY.RL.5.2: Determine a theme of a story, drama, or poem from details in the text, including how characters in a story or drama respond to challenges or how the speaker in a poem reflects upon a topic; summarize the text. CCSS.ELA-LITERACY.RL.5.6: Describe how a narrator's or speaker's point of view influences how events are described. CCSS.ELA-LITERACY.SL5.2: Summarize a written text read aloud or information presented in diverse media and formats, including visually, quantitatively, and orally.
Strand 2: Responding to Text • Questions that clarify, fortify, and extend ideas • Group responsibilities (follow rules, be prepared, etc.) • Strategies for active listening and responding • Types of connections	CCSS.ELA-LITERACY.SL.5.1.A: Come to discussions prepared, having read or studied required material; explicitly draw on that preparation or other information known about the topic, to explore ideas under discussion. CCSS.ELA-LITERACY.SL.5.1B: Follow agreed upon rules for discussions and carry out assigned roles. CCSS.ELA-LITERACY.SL.5.1C:Pose questions and respond to specific questions by making comments that contribute to the discussion and elaborate on the remarks of others. CCSS.ELA-LITERACY.SL.5.1D: Review key ideas expressed and draw conclusions in light of information and knowledge gained from the discussions.
Strand 3: Critiquing Text • Effectiveness of word choice • Qualities of author's craft in personal narratives • Definition of precise language • Elements of personal narratives	CCSS.ELA-LITERACY.RL.5.9: Compare and contrast stories in the same genre (e.g., mysteries and adventure stories) on their approaches to similar themes and topics. CCSS.ELA-LITERACY.W.5.1C: Link opinion and reasons using words, phrases, and clauses (e.g., consequently, specifically).
Strand 4: Producing Text • Stages of a writing process • Transitional words and phrases • Common elements of the genre • Effective narrative techniques • Text organization	CCSS.ELA-LITERACY.W.5.3: Write narratives to develop real or imagined experiences or events using effective technique, descriptive details, and clear event sequences. CCSS.ELA-LITERACY.W.5.3A: Orient reader by establishing a situation and introducing a narrator and/or characters; organize an event sequence that unfolds naturally. CCSS.ELA-LITERACY.W.5.3B: Use narrative techniques, such as dialogue, description, and pacing, to develop experiences and events or show the responses of characters to situations.

• Transition words • Meaning of writing precisely • Writing conventions • Definition of precise language, concrete words and phrases, and sensory details	CCSS.ELA-LITERACY.W.5.3C: Use a variety of transitional words, phrases, and clauses to manage the sequence of events. CCSS.ELA-LITERACY.W.5.3D: Use concrete words and phrases and sensory details to convey experiences and events precisely. CCSS.ELA-LITERACY.W.5.3E: Provide a conclusion that follows from the narrated experiences or events. CCSS.ELA-LITERACY.L.5.2: Demonstrate command of the conventions of standard English capitalization, punctuation, and spelling when writing. CCSS.ELA-LITERACY.L.5.3: A Expand, combine, and reduce sentences for meaning, reader/listener interest, and style.

Unit Title: *Personal Narratives: Here's My Story* **Conceptual Lens:** Genre/Author's Craft
Grade Level: 5

Suggested Timeline	Suggested Learning Experiences	Assessments	Differentiation	Resources

Thinking About Learning Experiences

In Model Unit 4, *Oh The Choices Authors Face!*, we asked you to consider the gradual release of responsibility and the transfer of ownership for learning from the teacher to the student.

You reflected on the following questions:

- What skill, strategy, or type of problem solving would best be taught through the gradual release of responsibility?
- What piece of mentor text or example that reflects the learning target could be used to model, by thinking aloud, the skill, strategy, or type of problem solving that students would be expected to utilize in their upcoming learning experience?
- How will you know when students are ready for independent practice?

Now let's think about this. . .

Student choice is a foundational aspect of Concept-Based literacy. Again, we aren't talking about carte blanche classroom choice; we are talking about looking for ways that allow students to be involved in decisions that will empower and inspire them as learners.

As you design learning for your students, how will you provide opportunities for students to make choices about,

- the texts they will read?
- the products they will produce?
- the learning goals to work toward?
- the topics they wish to write about?

Culminating Unit Assessment

Unit Title: *Personal Narratives: Here's My Story*
Grade Level: 5

Conceptual Lens: Author's Craft/Choice

What (the unit focus): Students will investigate personal narratives,

Why (the generalization or generalizations): in order to understand that . . .

Author's craft personal narratives so that readers feel they shared the same experience.

How (the engaging scenario for students):

Here's My Story Project:

As a fifth grader, who now has an understanding of how different authors craft personal narratives, you are ready to share your story.

First, you will brainstorm a title that identifies a life experience you are going to write about. Think about some of the titles authors in this unit used: My First Day at a New School, How I met my Best Friend, and so on.

Think about how you will organize your story (the text structure). For example, will you tell about the event sequentially or will you use a problem/solution structure?

Next you need to map out your story elements that we have learned in this unit: characters, setting, plot, pacing, change, significance. Now you are ready to begin your first draft of your personal narrative. Remember, you want to craft your story so that readers feel they share the same experience that you are describing. We learned about the ways authors do this so looking back through your writing journals, mentor texts, assignments, class anchor charts, and so on, may help. Once your narrative has moved through all the stages of your writing process, your published piece will be bound and recognized in our publishing celebration in the school library. Your personal narratives will be on display for a month for others to enjoy.

Also, after your story is published, I will be having individual writing conferences. During our conference, you will explain, citing examples from your narrative, the techniques you used to craft your story so that your readers would feel they shared your experience.

Scoring Guide

CRITERIA	4	3	2	1
Understanding				
Content: A.				
B.				
C.				
Process: A.				
B.				
C.				

Thinking About Scoring Guides

You've probably realized by now that there are no "right" or "wrong" answers in terms of how to design scoring guides. As long as students are assessed in terms of KUDs (what students **K**now (content knowledge), what they **U**nderstand (generalization), and what they are able to **D**o (process, strategies and skills), the style and structure of a scoring tool can vary.

Some school systems find it worthwhile to create a consistent format in scoring tools across grade levels, subject areas, or schools. Doing so across enables students to become more proficient at self-assessing because they are familiar with the format. Families may also appreciate the consistent method of communication.

Whether or not you design a more detailed rubric or a streamlined scoring tool, what is important is that it aligns with the expectations of the Culminating Unit Assessment and will help your students see what they did well and where improvements are needed.

Resource B-1 Sample Graphic Organizer for Deep Analysis of Text

Inquiry into Deep Analysis of Text

Title and Author of Text:____

What did you uncover in your novel through deep analysis of the text?

Writer's Craft—
(insert a question about a specific technique under study. For example, "What typeof allusion did the author use—Historical, Biblical, Literary, Cultural?")

Reader's Craft—
(insert a question about a reader's response to the specific technique under study. For example, "What strategies and skills did you use as a reader to make sense of this allusion?")

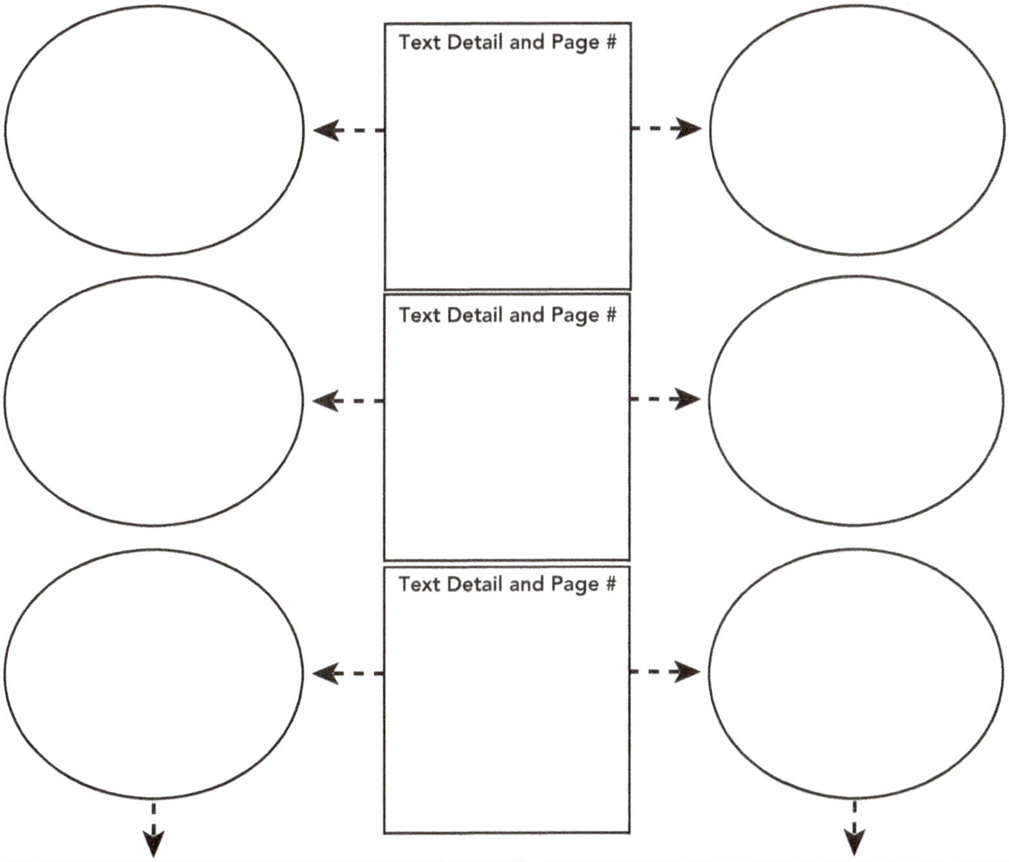

Writer's Craft: (write a question about the technique under study that will help lead students to the target generalization. For example, How do allusions in literature affect a reader?")

Write a generalization to show what you understand about _______ (for example, why writers use allusions). Finish the statement,"I understand that . . ."

Reader's Craft: (ask students to review the responses above. For example, Review the strategies and skills you used to uncover the identified allusions.)

Write a generalization showing the relationship between a reader and writer when ______(meaning is implied). Finish the statement, "I understand that . . ."

Resource B-2 Noticing Patterns Across Multiple Texts—Version A

How did the author of your book appeal to readers' senses?

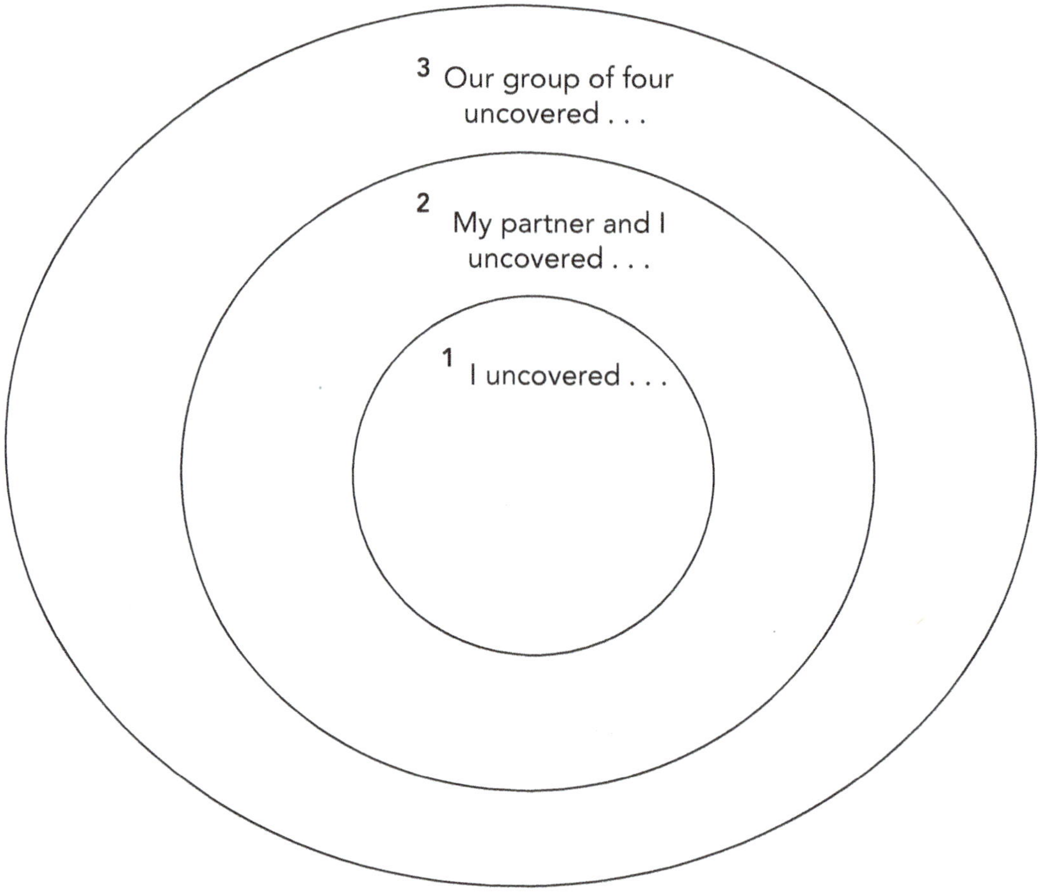

Steps:

1. In the center circle, write your answer to the guiding question.
2. Find a classmate. As a partner pair, discuss your answer to the guiding question. What do the two books have in common? Write the similarities in the second circle.
3. Find another partner pair. As a group of four, discuss that similarities that each partner pair uncovered. What patterns do you notice among the group of four? Write the similarities in the third circle.
4. Individually, write a generalization in the box below.

4

Generalization: *What do you now understand about the relationship between authors' word choice and creating images for the reader?*

I understand that . . .

Resource B-3 Noticing Patterns Across Multiple Texts—Version B

Guiding Question:___________________________________

Text 1:

Text 2:

All Texts

Text 3:

Text 4:

Based on what we've uncovered, what do you now understand about ________?

Resource B-4 Tracking Thinking Protocol

Tracking My Thinking

Create a web to capture your deepening understanding as you engage in the inquiry.

Initial Understanding:

What do you understand about the relationship between ________ and ________?

Steps:

- Capture your initial understanding in pencil
- After first case study, add new ideas/concepts in blue colored pencil
- After second case study, add new ideas/concepts in green colored pencil
- After third case study, add new ideas/concepts in red colored pencil
- At the end of the inquiry, review your web and reflect on how your thinking deepened over time. Craft a generalization to express what you now understand.

My Generalization
Now I understand that . . .

Resource C: Student Reflection and Self-Assessment of Process

Resource C-1 Student Reflection and Self-Assessment

Student Self-Reflection and Self-Assessment of Process in a Concept-Based Literacy Classroom

Providing opportunities for students to self-reflect and self-assess are common practices in most literacy classrooms. Teachers ask students to reflect on their work and to self-assess the overall quality of the result (often using a rubric or other scoring tool). For example, when students self-evaluate a piece of their writing, they better understand the strengths of the piece and where they can make improvements—this is valuable learning! Too often, however, students engage in the routine application of self-reflection and self-assessment of only product, not process. Students' understanding of why they are doing what they are doing or which strategies and skills resulted in better quality are not the focus.

Concept-Based Literacy instruction ensures students develop self-reflection and self-assessment habits of mind. Because literacy is a process-oriented discipline, students need an *understanding* of the essential strategies and skills necessary to achieve the intended result (comprehension, quality writing, effective speaking, and so on). This means teachers must frequently ask students to consider *what* they did as readers, writers, speakers, listeners, and viewers, and *why*. Here are two ways CBCI teachers support the development of students' literacy habits of mind:

Inductive Reflection and Self-Assessment:

Students reflect on the choices they are making during learning experiences that lead to a target generalization. In other words, students pause and explain why they are doing what they are doing as readers, writers, speakers, listeners, or viewers. The emphasis is on the strategies and skills required in a process (writing process, listening process, comprehension process, and so on). By periodically asking students to explain their actions, inductively they learn to become more conscious of their choices and how well the choices are working.

Deductive Self-Reflection and Self-Assessment:

In this situation, students already constructed the target generalization through carefully structured and sequenced teacher Guiding Questions and Learning Experiences. Now, students stand back and reflect on how the overall result was accomplished. What was accomplished depends on the wording of the target generalization. The students are now asked to go back and self-reflect and self-assess how well they did (against defined criteria) and what they did to achieve this result.

Generalizations	Inductive Approach *Occurs during the learning experiences leading to the construction of the target generalization*	Deductive Approach *Occurs after the target generalization is realized*
Description	Students reflect on the process, strategies, and skills they are applying to learning experiences designed to lead their thinking to a target generalization. Periodically the teacher pauses the student work and checks in on the process—not telling students what to do, but asking conceptual questions that require students to articulate why they are doing *what* they are doing.	Students reflect on the generalization (they derived from the learning experiences) and on the process, strategies, and skills they used to reach the targeted understanding. Students support their reflections with examples from their work as evidence that they can apply the generalization to new situations.
Examples of Questions to Ask Students to Provoke Reflection and Assessment	"How can you, as a memoir writer, put your readers into your story so they feel they are with you at this moment?" "How well are the strategies and skills you are using working? What else could you try?" "You are finding this to be challenging text. What strategies can you try?" "What are you noticing about your group participation?"	"Where is the evidence of the generalization in your work? Or, how does your work reflect the understanding in the generalization?" "What strategies and skills helped you successfully construct the generalization?" "Would you do anything differently next time?" "How did you know you were on the right track?" "How will you use these strategies and skills in new situations?"

Resource C-2 Teacher-Assigned Craft Reports as Assessments of Conceptual Understanding

Craft Reports often include written reflections of the literacy choices students make but go one step further. Craft Reports ask students to construct and articulate a *conceptual understanding* that reflects an important, transferable idea represented in their assigned tasks.

Teachers are very comfortable with assessing students' factual knowledge and skills, and most assessments stop there. An assessment of understanding is frequently missing. The primary purpose of a Craft Report is to ensure teachers are not making assumptions about students' reaching the *target generalization*. Craft Reports can serve as formative or summative assessments. When a teacher incorporates specific language from the generalization into the directions, students' thinking is guided toward a tighter, more focused response, which provides clear evidence of their conceptual understanding.

In the examples below, notice how Craft Report directions pick up language (underlined) from the target generalization. This is not the time to have students writing at length and veering off to include all that they learned throughout the lesson or unit. It is an assessment of a specific conceptual understanding we don't want to leave to chance.

Examples:

Target Generalization:
Short story writers deliberately limit dialogue and description to ensure action moves swiftly.

Assessment Directions with Craft Report:
After you complete your short story, write a Craft Report paragraph explaining how you as a writer deliberately limited dialogue and description in order to ensure action moved swiftly. Cite examples from your story.

Target Generalization:
Political cartoonist use specific techniques (symbolism, exaggeration, labeling) for the purpose of conveying a larger idea and/or advancing an opinion.

Assessment Directions with Craft Report:
Draw a political cartoon. Next, write a Craft Report explaining the specific techniques you used and explain the purpose of your cartoon. Finally, write a generalization that expresses the relationship among the concepts: Political Cartoonists—Techniques—Purpose

The non-example below is not an assessment of conceptual understanding. Why? Even if a student were to write a well-constructed mystery story, we cannot assume the product means understanding has been internalized. Assessments of conceptual understanding require an active *linguistic* and *cognitive* response from students. We can "hear" how a student's understanding develops over time. If a person truly understands, then he/she should be able to articulate what is understood. If this is not the case, it is very likely that when learning expectations get more complex and challenging, performance will falter because understanding was not truly there.

Non-Example:

Target Generalization:
Mystery writers focus plot action on a central character and suspects, and insert clues and red herrings into a conflict with heightening tension to create an engaging, suspenseful piece of literature.

Assessment Directions:
We have read many mysteries throughout the course of this unit. Now it is your turn! Write your "Who Done It!" story to share with classmates.

Excerpt from a Craft Report:

"I used counterarguments in my writing to show the opinions of the other side. What I then did in response to the counterarguments was address why their argument is invalid against my claim. This made my argument much stronger."

—Eighth Grade Concept-Based Student

Resource C-3 Sample Reflection and Self-Assessment

Socratic Seminar Self-Reflection and Self-Assessment

Part A: Reflect on your process during our Socratic Seminar

1. *How did you feel about your participation in the seminar? Did you participate more this time than the last time that you engaged in a Socratic Seminar?*

2. *Is there anything you wish you had said?*

3. *What did someone say during your group conversation that caused you to think differently about the topic?*

4. *What role does discourse have in understanding a text?*

5. *Why is it necessary to revise thinking?*

Part B: Self-Assessment

Score yourself by highlighting, underlining, or circling characteristics in the different columns on the rubric below. See which column includes most of your responses. What will you do differently next time?

Meeting Expectations	Making Progress	Developing
I came prepared with extensive evidence and higher order questions. I asked at least one question that provoked discussion or initiated a new topic that propelled our thinking forward. I contributed to the discussion, helped deepen our thinking, and built on the ideas of others. I referenced evidence from readings as I was sharing and others were sharing. I ensured all voices were heard in the discussion by inviting a classmate to share their ideas. I paid close attention to the discussion and remained focused the entire time.	I came prepared with a question and some evidence. I asked at least one question or initiated a new topic. I made relevant contributions to the discussion a couple times. At times, I referenced evidence as I was sharing, and when others were sharing. I mostly paid attention in the discussion, but may have lost focus once or twice.	My preparation was minimal. I was quiet throughout the discussion and let others make all the contributions. Sometimes I paid attention in the discussion, but I often lost focus or engaged in a side conversation.

Resource D: Other Tools to Support Concept-Based Literacy Lesson Design

Resource D-1 Sample Literary Concepts

Examples of Concepts in Literacy Compiled by Dr. Lois A. Lanning and Tiffanee Brown, 2018

Concepts in Text (Print, film, multimedia, speeches, illustrations)	Receptive Concepts (Reader's/Listener's/Viewer's Craft)		Expressive Concepts (Writer's/Speaker's/Presenter's Craft)	
Power Identity Survival Fear Inner/outer conflict Courage Love Relationships Loss Friendships Caring/Sharing Jealousy Tolerance Idealism Isolationism Greed Sacrifice Compromise Control Justice Humanity/ Inhumanity Elements of genre Sample Conceptual Lenses Relationships Conflict Inference Text Structure Intent Argumentation Theme Text Features Language Perspectives Characterization Craft Genre Research Patterns Deconstruction Process Influence Persuasion Voice Identity Choices Expression Mood Form	**Understanding/ Comprehension (of text)** Main idea/Central idea Summary Strategies/Skills Directionality Phonological awareness Phonics Self-regulation Problem solving Metacognition Self-correction Reading rate Text language/ vocabulary Inference Context clues Connections Imagery Organization Text structure Cause/effect Problem/solution Chronological Sequence Narrative Text features Text medium Background knowledge Purpose Aesthetic pleasure Information Entertainment Explanation Research Theme Deep text analysis Claim Story elements Character Protagonist Antagonist Traits Narrator Plot Setting Conflict External Internal Dialogue Resolution Point of view Text type (genre) Literary analysis	**Response (to text)** Questions Connections Point of View Reflection Discourse protocols Collaboration Perspective Conclusions Personal reflection Interpretation Text evidence Cultural understanding Motivation/appeal Active listening Feedback Precise expression Reader response Individual and group responsibilities Background knowledge Paraphrase **Critiquing Text** Author's craft Critical stance Literary criticism Evaluation Judgment Believability Appreciation/recognition of author's craft Relevance Emphasis Credibility Currency Relevance Validity Accuracy Evidence Reasoning Logic Ethos Pathos Logos Fallacy Bias Effectiveness of exposition or argument Precise language Impact Clarity Style Similarities/ differences	**Production (of text)** Voice Tone Mood Dialect Style Organization Thesis Transitions Text structure Leads Details Elaboration Fluency Rhythm Cadence Flow Sentence structure Syntax Writing/speaking conventions Grammar Language (formal/informal) Mechanics Format Visual representation/ Graphic Multimedia Medium Layout Font Narrative elements Characterization Word choice/usage Precise language Concrete detail Sensory detail Connotation Audience awareness Appeal Persuasive techniques Argumentation Counter arguments Oracy/ Speaker Pitch Pause Volume Rhythm Intonation Rhetorical device	**Production (of text) continued** Literary devices Epithets Epigrams Alliteration Hyperbole Imagery Allegory Metaphor Allusion Figurative language Simile Onomatopoeia Symbolism Writing Process Brainstorm Draft Edit Response Revision Publication Reflection ***Concepts Range in Specificity*** *More Broad* ↓ Author's Craft Literary Device Allusion *More Precise* *Microconcepts Increase Depth and Add Precision*

Resource D-2 Two-Dimensional Versus Three-Dimensional Literacy *at a Glance*

Common Characteristics of Two-Dimensional Literacy		Characteristics of Three-Dimensional Literacy
All students read the same text	← - - - - →	Teacher provides multiple texts to give students choice, to encourage students to identify patterns across texts, and to provide access to texts at the appropriate level of readability and interest.
Focus on mastering skills, strategies, or processes	← - - - - →	Focus on mastering skills, strategies, and processes while also moving beyond the standard to develop understanding of concepts important to the discipline. Students move from simply "doing" skills to understanding the "why" and "how" behind practices.
Questions remain at the factual or knowledge level	← - - - - →	Factual, conceptual, and sometimes debatable, guiding questions engage synergistic thinking and path students' thinking to the understanding in the generalizations.
Units and lessons do not have a conceptual lens	← - - - - →	A conceptual lens focuses and directs thinking.
Learning is locked to a specific text or specific activity	← - - - - →	Learning is not locked to a specific text or assignment as conceptual understanding transfers to other situations. Learning through concepts develops schemata in the brain which act as building blocks for new learning.
Skills are often taught in isolation; learning is often a series of disconnected activities	← - - - - →	Learning experiences, drawn from a cohesive curriculum unit, represent a guided inquiry approach while addressing what students must Know, Understand, and be able to Do (skills). Instruction may Pause & Zoom-in on specific skills as needed, but the more complex, authentic learning experience, where the skills will be applied, is never out of sight for long.
Learning targets are directly stated before engaging in the lesson	← - - - - →	Lessons often start with a conceptual question or scenario designed to provoke curiosity, or activate students' synergistic thinking.
Teaching a text with focused attention on the author, content, and form of the work	← - - - - →	Teaching focuses on the readers, writers, listeners, speakers, and viewers ongoing transaction or interplay with text and on developing an understanding of how language works.
Primarily deductive learning design	← - - - - →	Blends inductive and deductive learning design
Reflection is often limited to goal setting, or reflecting about a product	← - - - - →	Students reflect on their individual progress, the processes, strategies, and skills they are using, AND on their developing understanding of the major concepts and ideas essential to the discipline of English Language Arts.

Resource D-3 Before-You-Teach Quick Check

Concept-Based Instruction *Quick Check*

Lesson Opening:

- Captivating overview connects and extends previous learning
- Immediately engages students' minds and interests
- Ignites synergistic thinking by asking students to consider the knowledge and/or skills they will be learning through a conceptual question(s) or lens

During Lesson:

- Creates synergistic thinking through instructional techniques and thought-provoking examples
- Student work requires students to cognitively wrestle with and synthesize the knowledge, skills, and concepts under study in relevant contexts that lead to the realization of the generalization
- Learning experiences and resources bridge to a deeper, conceptual understanding
- Teaching uses a variety of techniques to support the transfer of learning and deepening of understanding (for example, questioning, asking for other examples/non-examples of the same concept or generalizations, ongoing feedback, and by asking students to express an analysis of their reasoning with supporting evidence)
- A gradual release of responsibility and ownership for learning from teacher to the student is clear
- Continuous monitoring of students' independent and collaborative group work with timely, relevant feedback and questions that facilitate & mediate the learning process

Lesson Closing:

- Evidence of learning (formative or summative) is collected about students' progress toward the lesson's targeted knowledge, skills, and understanding
- Teacher and students reflect on and analyze the success of the learning (process and product)
- Students learn how the learning will build toward future learning targets

Adapted From: The Developing Concept-Based Teacher: Concept-Based Instruction Rubric (Lanning, 2013)

Resource E-1 Understanding of Concept-Based Curriculum and Instruction Rubric

The Developing Concept-Based Teacher: *Understanding of Concept-Based Curriculum and Instruction*

	Novice	Emerging	Master
Support for Concept Based	*Names one or two reasons for Concept-Based teaching and learning	*Articulates the major reasons for concept-based teaching and learning	*Articulates the reasons for Concept-Based Curriculum and Instruction citing relevant supporting research
Components of Concept-Based: *Concepts (macro-micro)* *Conceptual Lens* *Synergistic Thinking* *Generalizations* *Guiding Questions leveled & aligned with generalizations* *Critical Knowledge & Key Skills* *Performance assessments versus activities*	*Can define some of the elements of a 3-Dimensional Concept-Based curriculum model versus a 2-C Dimensional model *From a list of concepts, distinguishes macro- from micro-concepts *Can define synergistic thinking but cannot yet explain methods to create synergistic thinking among students.	*Uses correct Concept-Based terminology but may not be clear about the rationale for each component *When reviewing Concept-Based Curriculum and/or Instruction, recognizes the 3-Dimensional components *Explains the difference between macro- and micro-concepts and states why it is important to know the difference *Defines synergistic thinking and gives at least one example of an instructional technique/strategy for engaging students' synergistic thinking	*Explains the various components of Concept-Based Curriculum using correct terminology and the rationale for each *When reviewing a 2-Dimensional curriculum and/or lesson, suggests changes that will move the curriculum or lesson to a 3-Dimensional model *Demonstrates a solid understanding of macro- and micro-concepts by explaining how to employ them accurately and effectively in Concept-Based Curriculum & Instruction *Can explain the value of synergistic thinking and offers more than one personally created example of instructional techniques/strategies that clearly engage students' synergistic thinking
Commitment to Continued Learning	*Participates in Concept-Based presentations and attempts steps to adapt 2-Dimensional lessons to 3-Dimensional lessons	*Participates in professional development presentations on Concept-Based and follows up by attempting to put new learning into practice *Accepts formal or informal coaching and mentoring support *Independently reads texts on Concept-Based Curriculum and Instruction	*Passionately supports Concept-Based as evidenced by active participation in presentations or book study groups with follow-up implementation that includes ongoing communication and collaborative work with others (for example, coaching and mentoring) *Demonstrates continued effort to deepen understanding through sharing learning and leading professional development *Continually reflects upon and refines practice

Resource E-2 Concept-Based Lesson Planning Rubric

The Developing Concept-Based Teacher: *Concept-Based Lesson Planning*

Components of Lesson Plan	Novice	Emerging	Master
Lesson Opening: *An explicit and engaging summary of the work to be accomplished that triggers synergistic thinking*	*Lesson opens by stating the activities students will experience in the lesson and may include stating the generalization the lesson will be teaching toward	*Lesson opening contains a conceptual lens, but the weak tie to content fails to engage synergistic thinking	*The lesson opening engages synergistic thinking by asking students to consider the knowledge and/or skills they will be learning through a conceptual question(s) or lens
Learning targets: *What students are expected to Know (factual knowledge), Understand (generalization), and be able to Do (skills)*	*What students must Know and/or be able to Do) is listed in the lesson plan	*Targets identify what students must Know, Understand (generalization), and Do, but there may be more learning targets than can be accomplished in-depth within the lesson time frame	*Learning targets represent what students are expected to Know, Understand, and Do; the limited number of learning targets allows for in-depth, focused instruction and learning
Guiding Questions: *The three different types of questions (factual, conceptual, debatable) serve as a bridging tool for conceptual thinking and problem solving.*	*Questions in the lesson plan focus heavily on factual knowledge and routine skills	*Lesson questions reflect different types (factual, conceptual, and possibly debatable questions) and anticipate student misconceptions	*Potential questions are of different types (factual, conceptual, provocative) and are listed throughout the plan *The lesson plan shows a deliberate effort to use questions to help students bridge from the factual to the conceptual level of understanding
Learning Experiences: *Intellectually engaging student work that provide opportunities for students to practice their learning and to arrive at the target generalization (conceptual understanding)*	*The targeted knowledge and skills are indicated in the plan, but the learning experiences do not require students to apply their learning in relevant contexts, which would clearly lead to conceptual understanding and transfer across learning situations *The student work required in the lesson primarily relies on worksheets, disconnected skills, and facts that are not authentic or intellectually/emotionally engaging for students	*The student work attempts to pursue conceptual understandings but may not provide a clear pathway with enough examples or scaffolds for students to realize the conceptual understanding (generalization) *Lesson plan shows efforts to design student work to engage students' interest and offers some student choice *Assignments are intellectually and emotionally engaging but are not at the appropriate level of challenge for all students	*The student work requires students to cognitively wrestle with and synthesize the knowledge, skills. and concepts under study in relevant contexts that lead to the realization of the generalization *Student work is at the appropriate level of challenge, is intellectually and emotionally engaging, meaningful and relevant to the discipline, and provides appropriate student choice *The learning experiences are deliberately designed to enhance the transfer of learning across other disciplines and situations

Components of Lesson Plan	Novice	Emerging	Master
Assessment methods: *Assessment types are selected according to the lesson's learning targets (Know, Understand, Do) and to the assessment purposes (formative and summative) in order to capture evidence of students' learning (process and product), which will then inform instruction.*	*Assessment types are limited so it is difficult to know the degree of students' learning and progress toward conceptual understanding	*Assessment types are varied and help monitor students' developing knowledge and skills *Assessments of understanding, aligned to the target generalization, are not clear	*Assessment types are varied so that they assess students' developing knowledge, skills, and understandings (generalization) and allow for timely feedback *Assessments provide relevant information about students' process of learning as well as their learning products *Student self-assessment is valued
Differentiation: *Lesson adjustments are planned, as needed, for the content students are expected to master, the process students will use to access the content, and the product students will produce to show their learning. The conceptual understanding (generalization) all students are expected to realize remains consistent for all students.*	*Plans for differentiation may be stated but lack relevance to individual student learning needs	*Plans for differentiation are included for students who need support (special education, ELL, and so on) in the areas of content, process, and product *Misconceptions are generally addressed for the class as a whole	*Plans for differentiation to meet the needs of all learners are included and support all students' meeting a common conceptual understanding (generalization) *Differentiation is based on an analysis of multiple data points that reveal individual students' learning needs *Specific accommodations are readily available based on anticipated student misconceptions and needs

(Continued)

Resource E-2 (Continued)

Components of Lesson Plan	Novice	Emerging	Master
Lesson Design: *In a deductive lesson design, the teacher states the learning targets (including generalization) to the learners at the beginning of the instruction. In an inductive design, students construct their understandings through an inquiry process.*	*The lesson design is deductive (for example, objective to example vs. example to generalization)	*The lesson design attempts to use inductive teaching but the examples presented only vaguely illustrate the targeted conceptual understandings *A deductive design may also be included to support the learning of foundational facts and skills	*The lesson design is primarily inductive, requiring students to engage in a multifaceted inquiry process, and to reflect on the connections across the examples presented so that students can formulate and defend their generalizations *A deductive design may also be included to support the learning of foundational facts and skills
Closing: *Plan for how the lesson will be collectively summarized with opportunities for reflection on process, product, and transfer before setting up where learning will go next.*	*A summary statement of the lesson is planned	*A summary statement of the lesson is planned *An assignment is created for practicing the knowledge and skills of the lesson *The next steps in learning are determined	*There is a plan for collaboratively summarizing the lesson, making connections to previous learning, and accounting for transfer *Time is allotted for students to reflect on their product and process *The next steps in learning are determined *An assignment may be created that extends or reinforces the lesson's learning targets

Resource E-3 Concept-Based Instruction Rubric

The Developing Concept-Based Teacher: *Concept-Based Instruction*

	Novice	Emerging	Master
Lesson Opening	*Lesson opens by launching directly into an activity without providing an overview or clear directions *The lesson's target generalization is posted or stated at the beginning of the lesson rather than drawn from students throughout *The lesson opening is accurate but bland and leaves students disinterested as it is more of a teacher monologue	*The lesson opening sets the stage for inductive teaching that will draw out conceptual understandings from the students (e.g., examples are posted, intriguing questions presented, an interesting scenario shared, relevant concepts posed, etc.) but the opening is overly detailed and too long	*The opening clearly communicates an engaging, captivating overview of the lesson that connects and extends previous learning *The lesson immediately engages students' minds and interests
During: Instruction reflects modeling, facilitating, and mediating conceptual understanding	*The lesson follows the written lesson plan, but since the plan does not address all the elements of an effective Concept-Based lesson, instruction falls short *Concepts are somewhat apparent in the lesson, with little attention of how to use concepts to create intellectual engagement and deepen students' understanding *Focus is less on the transfer of learning and more on task completion *Instruction employs different kinds of questions as the main tool for encouraging the transfer of learning but still overrelies on factual questions	*Follows the Concept-Based lesson plan prescriptively *Maintains the emotional engagement of students by using examples and resources that resonate with students' interests and concerns, and invite deeper intellectual engagement, but students' assigned work and instructional techniques do not clearly lead students to synergistic thinking (moving examples to related concepts) *Instruction is somewhat responsive to flashes of quality student thinking, but uses limited strategies for encouraging and guiding deeper conceptual understanding and transfer	*The execution of the lesson plan is well paced, while being flexible and responsive to anticipated student needs (and needs that arise throughout the lesson) *There is conscious and consistent development of students' synergistic thinking through instructional techniques and thought-provoking examples and through learning experiences and resources that bridge to a deeper, conceptual idea (understanding) *Teaching uses a variety of techniques to support the transfer of learning and deepening of understanding (e.g., questioning, asking for other examples/non-examples of the same concept or generalizations, feedback, and by asking students for an analysis of their reasoning with supporting evidence) *Gradual release of responsibility and ownership for learning from teacher to student is clear

(*Continued*)

Resource E-3 (Continued)

	Novice	Emerging	Master
	*Instruction remains predominately teacher-centered *Student participation is predominately in response to teacher questioning and evaluation	*There is some gradual release of responsibility of learning from teacher to student, but the teacher is assuming most of the cognitive work *Most students are engaged in the learning while clusters of students may remain off-task or disinterested due to ineffective level of challenge or lack of relevance	*Continuous monitoring of students' independent and collaborative group work with timely, relevant feedback and questions that facilitate and mediate the learning process
Lesson Closing	*The teacher recaps the learning experiences in the lesson	*There is a closing assessment (formative or summative) of the knowledge, skills students learned, and an attempt to determine students' level of conceptual understanding *Relevant practice beyond the lesson is assigned	*Evidence of learning (formative or summa- tive) the lesson's targeted knowledge, skills, and understandings is collected *Collaboratively the teacher and students reflect and analyze the success of the learning (process and product) *Students learn how the learning will build toward future learning targets

Resource E-4 Developing Concept-Based Student Rubric

The Developing Concept-Based Student Rubric

Attributes	Novice	Emerging	Advanced
Task Commitment	*Views work as compliance versus ownership of task *Tasks are seen as separate and unrelated *May become impatient and easily frustrated *Stays within the guidelines of the assignment	*Sees the learning relevance of assigned work *Stays clearly focused and self-regulated throughout task *Willing to persevere through challenges that are within reach *Accepts responsibility for work *Actively participates in collaborative groups *May incorporate new directions or approaches to an assignment	*Independently seeks to extend the assigned work *Expresses enthusiasm and genuine interest in the challenge of the work *Demonstrates self-discipline and persistence with longer term and more complex work *Values and seeks collaboration to complete task *Is as interested in the learning process as producing a quality product
Synergistic Thinking	*Recognizes connections and patterns among ideas or solutions when they are pointed out *Inconsistently ties concepts to the presented examples *Makes generalizations that are overly simplified	*Synthesizes information into a coherent generalization *Supports generalization with at least two accurate examples *Links factual examples to presented concepts	*Transforms examples and ideas into higher-level generalizations *Articulates generalization and clearly supports with multiple examples *Independently links factual examples to related concepts and/or generalizations. *Independently provides examples and non-examples of concepts *Thought process shows unique and inventive connections between generalizations, concepts, examples, and product

(Continued)

Resource E-4 (Continued)

Attributes	Novice	Emerging	Advanced
Depth of Understanding	*Needs support with attempts to explain learning targets, thinking, and/or generalizations *Generates relevant questions, but most are still at the factual level	*Clearly explains personal position and acknowledges other perspectives *Produces thoughtful, detailed products *Formulates relevant questions *Incorporates prior learning into present context *Transfers generalizations across a few concrete examples *Expanding use of conceptual language in explanations *Recognizes non-examples of concepts	*Systematically and methodically explains understanding supported by relevant evidence *Creates novel products *Creates new knowledge by extending ideas, experimenting with product guidelines, applying different learning strategies *Shows the ability to prioritize and critique the relevance of examples *Transfers generalization across multiple, more complex examples *Uses conceptual language confidently and accurately *Independently provides examples and non-examples of concepts

References

Bransford, J. D., Brown, A. L., & Cocking, R. R. (Eds.). (1999). *How people learn: Brain, mind, experience, and school.* Washington, DC: National Academies Press.

Erickson, H. L. (2008). *Stirring the head, heart, and soul: Redefining curriculum, instruction, and concept-based learning* (3rd ed.). Thousand Oaks, CA: Corwin.

Erickson, H. L., & Lanning, L. A. (2014) *Transitioning to concept-based curriculum and instruction: How to bring content and process together.* Thousand Oaks, CA: Corwin.

Erickson, H. L., Lanning, L. A., & French, R. (2017). *Concept-based curriculum and instruction for the thinking classroom* (2nd ed.). Thousand Oaks, CA: Corwin.

Fisher, D., Frey, N., & Hattie, J. (2016). *Visible learning for literacy.* Thousand Oaks, CA: Corwin.

Fisher, D., Frey, N., Hattie, J., & Thayre, M. (2017). *Teaching literacy in the visible learning classroom, grades 6–12.* Thousand Oaks, CA: Corwin.

Gallagher, K. (2003). *Reading reasons: Motivational mini-lessons for middle and high school.* Portland, ME: Stenhouse.

Hammond, Z. (2015). *Culturally responsive teaching and the brain: Promoting authentic engagement and rigor among culturally and linguistically diverse students.* Thousand Oaks, CA: Corwin.

Hattie, J. A. (2009). *Visible learning: A synthesis of over 800 meta-analyses relating to achievement.* New York, NY: Routledge.

Killian, S. (2017, January 18). Hattie effect size 2016 update. http://servelearn.co/wp-content/uploads/2017/02/evidencebasedteaching.org.au-Hattie-Effect-Size-2016-Update-Service-Learning.pdf

Lanning, L. A. (2009). *Four powerful strategies for struggling readers, grades 3–8: Small group instruction that improves comprehension.* Thousand Oaks, CA: Corwin.

Lanning, L. A. (2011). Gradual release to accelerate progress. In L. Laud (Ed.), *The best of Corwin: Differentiated instruction in literacy, math, and science* (pp. 23–30). Thousand Oaks, CA: Corwin.

Lanning, L. A. (2013). *Designing a concept-based curriculum for English language arts: Meeting the Common Core with intellectual integrity, K–12.* Thousand Oaks, CA: Corwin.

Marschall, C., & French, R. (2018). *Concept-based inquiry in action.* Thousand Oaks, CA: Corwin.

McLuhan, M. (1964). *Understanding the media: The extensions of man.* New York, NY: McGraw-Hill.

Means, B., & Knapp, M. S. (1991). Rethinking teaching for disadvantaged students. In B. Means, C. Chelemar, & M. S. Knapp (Eds.), *Teaching advanced skills to at-risk students: Views from research and practice* (pp. 1–26). San Francisco, Josey Bass.

Perkins, D. N., & Salomon, G. (1988). Teaching for transfer. *Educational Leadership, 46*(1), 22–32.

Smarter Balanced Assessment Consortium. (2015). *Assessment writing rubrics, grades 6–11.* UC Santa Cruz: The Regents of the University of California.

Index

Confident Teachers, Inspired Learners

H. LYNN ERICKSON, LOIS A. LANNING, RACHEL FRENCH

A Concept-Based Curriculum developed with the help of this book yields skillful, motivated students who can transfer knowledge and understanding to new situations along their learning journey.

H. LYNN ERICKSON, LOIS A. LANNING

Two renowned authors combine their expertise to show educators how to abandon rote teaching techniques and embrace Concept-Based Curriculum and its emphasis on critical thinking and analysis.

H. LYNN ERICKSON

This third edition of H. Lynn Erickson's bestseller provides updated information about designing curriculum aligned with state and national content standards, using brain-based teaching methods, and developing higher-order thinking skills.

LOIS A. LANNING

Fusing H. Lynn Erickson's groundbreaking curriculum model with implementation guidelines and sample units, this book puts you on the fast track to using Concept-Based Curriculum.

To order your copies, visit corwin.com

No matter where you are in your professional journey, Corwin aims to ease the many demands teachers face on a daily basis with accessible strategies that benefit ALL learners. Through research- based, high-quality content, we offer practical guidance on a wide range of topics, including curriculum planning, learning frameworks, classroom design and management, and much more. Our books, videos, consulting, and online resources are developed by renowned educators and designed for easy implementation that will provide tangible results for you and your students.

JENNIFER T. H. WATHALL

When you make the transition to concept-based teaching—using Jennifer T. H. Wathall's unit planners, templates, assessments, student work, and website resources—suddenly math makes sense to your students.

CARLA MARSCHALL, RACHEL FRENCH

Concept-Based Inquiry in Action provides teachers with the tools and resources necessary to facilitate the construction and transfer of conceptual understanding in any K–12 classroom.

JULIE STERN, NATHALIE LAURIAULT, KRISTA FERRARO

Concept-Based teaching helps students uncover conceptual relationships and transfer them to new contexts. Written for elementary educators, this is a must-have road map for implementing Concept-Based teaching.

JULIE STERN, KRISTA FERRARO, JULIET MOHNKERN

Discover how to help secondary learners uncover conceptual relationships and transfer them to new situations. With this foundation, students will be poised to become experts and innovators!

CORWIN

N18BG4

ACO 356395